CHANN

FAST
TO THE BARGAINS

RED WINE LESS THAN £1.00
go to page 98

WHITE WINE LESS THAN £1.00
go to page 98

ROSÉ WINE LESS THAN £1.00
go to page 98

SPARKLING WINE LESS THAN £1.00
go to page 98

CHAMPAGNE LESS THAN £6.00
go to page 98

BEER FROM 11p PER BOTTLE
go to page 110

SPIRITS - THE TIPPLE TABLE
go to page 99

The
Channel Hopper's
Guide

© 1998 by Passport Guide Publications

PO Box 336, Edgware, Middx HA8 8NL

Written By:	Sharron Livingston
Published By:	Passport Guide Publications
Business Manager:	Richard Abels
Enquiries :	0181 905 4851

*Very special thanks to Andrew Jefford, Wine Writer
for The Evening Standard, for his contribution to
The Channel Hopper's Guide wine tasting
and subsequent recommendations*

*Thanks also to Steven Bogen & Teresa Garfield
for their help and inspiration*

ISBN: 0 9524319 4 7

Contents

Contents

Introduction

Since the British Public has been taxed into sobriety, millions of people have taken to hopping across the Channel to take advantage of the huge savings that the French outlets offer.

Everyone knows that shopping for beers, wines, spirits and tobacco is much cheaper in France. However, it's not common knowledge that many other products are also substantially cheaper; for instance, did you know that mustard is at least 25% less than in the UK?

And it's not just food. Some makes of kitchenware, for example Tefal and Le Creuset, are half the price in France and huge savings can be made on a variety of hardware and garden products.

We at the Channel Hopper's Guide have done all the legwork for you, so you'll know exactly where to go and what is worthwhile to buy, which means you'll be buying the best products at the best prices available.

And if you're staying for a night or two, we have even made some hotel suggestions. But best of all, we have negotiated lots of exclusive special offers available only to you our readers, making your cross-Channel trip even better value for money!

So, whether you are looking to buy beer in bulk, cater for a special party or wedding, or stock up on your favourite tipples on your way home from your Continental holiday, make sure to keep the Channel Hopper's Guide with you. Just slip it into your passport wallet. You'll find, conveniently, it's exactly the same size.

Bon

Voyage

Hopping Over

Cross-Channel hopping has become a familiar aspect of British life with five companies all vying for custom by emphasising their own benefits.

The ferries have their own cruise appeal with extensive catering facilities. P&O & Stena Line pander to the British taste in food and SeaFrance being a French owned company, promote the French ambience and cuisine on board. The Hovercraft, owned by Hoverspeed, is a far more functional quick dash across the Channel and is a seafaring mode of air travel hovering just above the water on a bed of air. On board there are hostesses offering you the opportunity to buy duty free and drinks while you are seated. The Seacat catamaran, another Hoverspeed seafarer vehicle is a mix of ferry and Hovercraft.

The most recent addition to cross-Channel travel is Le Shuttle. It does not cater for foot passengers, but drivers enjoy a quick check-in and the convenience of train travel. You remain seated in your car in a carriage along with around five other cars. You may leave your car and walk the length of the carriage if you wish.

One thing is for sure, the cost of cross-Channel travel is very competitive. All five companies offer competitive deals throughout the year, and some even offer crossings for £1.00 (for foot passengers) through the national press in the hope of cashing in on increased duty free sales. It therefore makes good sense to shop around before you travel.

Better still, delegate this by joining a travel club. They exist to put together competitive travel packages and deals and will always offer the most competitive cross-Channel fare available. Try The Travel Club or EuroSave Travel.

Hopping Over

Five companies now cross the Channel to Calais/Boulogne.
Here is a resumé of their services to help you choose.

Crossing	From/To	Journey Time	Frequency	Duty Free
Stena Line: Tel: 01233 647047 Bus service to the town centre	Dover/Calais Check-in 30 mins	90 mins	Every 45 mins peak time	Yes - on board
P&O Ferries: Tel: 0990 980980 Bus service to Calais town centre	Dover/Calais Check-in 30 mins	75 mins 45 mins	Every 45 mins peak time	Yes - on board
Hoverspeed: Hovercraft Tel: 01304 240 241 Bus service to Railway Station. Fare: 50p	Dover/Calais Check-in 20 20 mins	35 mins	Every hour peak time	Yes - on board
Seacat: Tel: 01304 240 241	Folkestone/ Boulogne Check-in 30 mins	55 mins	Every hour peak time	Yes - on board
Le Shuttle: Tel: 0990 353535 No foot passengers. Vehicles only.	Folkestone/ Calais Turn up & go Check-in 20 mins	35 mins	Every 15 mins peak time	At the terminal only
SeaFrance: Tel: 0990 711711 Free bus service to Calais Town Centre	Dover/ Calais Check-in 30 mins	90 mins	Every 90 mins peak time	Yes - on board

Channel Travel Radio

**More of the information you need
as you travel to France.**

As you drive along the M20, head towards your ferry or prepare to board Le Shuttle, be sure to tune in to **Channel Travel Radio.** 107.6FM is the frequency to find if you want to hear all the very latest cross-channel travel information.

Channel Travel Radio broadcasts live, 24 hours a day from Le Shuttle's control centre in Folkestone. Tune in and you'll hear up-to-the-minute shuttle and ferry departure information, the latest continental weather forecasts and news about the conditions on Europe's roads. There are also lots of ideas on places to visit and things to do while you're abroad as well as a great selection of music.

If you'd like a special request on
the station, you can write to
Channel Travel Radio,
PO Box 2000, Folkestone,
Kent CT18 8XY
or call **01303 283823**.

What About Duty Free?

How Much Duty Free Can You Bring Back ?

The most important thing to be aware of is that you have the opportunity to purchase Duty Free on both outward and return journeys. This doubles your allowance if you take advantage on each leg of you journey; You cannot buy twice as much on a single leg as this contravenes the regulations. This does not affect your purchases in France Your Duty Free limits are:

Available on outward bound and return journeys

Duty Free Product	Outward	Return
Cigars or	50g	50g
Cigarettes or	200	200
Cigarillos or	100	100
Tobacco	250g	250g
Spirits & Liquers (over 22% volume)	1 Litre	1 Litre
Wine & Liquers (under 22% volume)	2 Litres	2 Litres
Still Table Wine	2 Litres	2 Litres
Beer/Gifts	up to £71	up to £71
Perfume &	60ml	60ml
Toilet Water	250ml	250ml

Duty Free Compared

Smokers, we recommend that you use up your duty free allowance.Top up at any Tabac (French newsagent). Duty Free is the cheapest place to purchase perfumes.Spirit drinkers can also benefit at Duty Free.

Some examples of popular drinks

	AVERAGE PRICES IN £ STERLING		
Product	Duty Free	France	UK
Baileys	12.25	11.90	16.70
Bells	9.60	14.28	17.55
Beefeater	9.95	12.99	17.12
Courvoisier ***	15.00	21.40	24.99
Jameson	11.45	14.91	19.70
Malibu	10.75	9.00	15.55
Bacardi	9.75	11.49	15.00
Pimms	9.95	13.21	16.84
Southern Comfort	13.10	19.78	21.69

Please note: Bottles usually sold in 70cl. have been calculated on quantities of 1 litre in order to show true like for like comparison with the Duty Free.

An interesting observation is that Duty Free whisky is 43% alcohol as opposed to the usual high street Scotch which is 40%.

What About Duty Free?

How Much Can You Bring Back From France
Go ahead stock up. But do not go over the top. If your purchases exceed the Advisory Guidelines, as set by customs and excise, you could be stopped.

Since 1 January 1993, you are permitted to bring back as much alcohol and tobacco as you like but it must be for personal use only. So you can happily stock up for

Christmas or a party or wedding reception. You are not, however, allowed to resell or barter the products. Although H M Customs and Excise have no authority to limit the amount you bring into this country they do have the right to stop you if your purchases exceed the 'Advisory Guidelines'. In this case you may be required to prove that the goods are for your own personal use.

The Advisory Guidelines are as follows:

Advisory Guidelines

Wine (*not to exceed 60 litres of sparkling wine*)	90 litres
Spirits	10 litres
Intermediate products (i.e. port and sherry)	20 litres
Beer	100 litres
Cigarettes	800
Cigarillos	400
Cigars	200
Tobacco	1 Kilogram

If you are stopped, remember that the H M Customs Officer is looking for bootleggers or those intent on resale and your co-operation will be appreciated. Other products such as mineral water, olives or any other non-alcoholic products, are not limited in anyway.

Remember
Your purchases made in France are not
affected by your duty free purchases

Focus on Folkestone

With the advent of the Chunnel Tunnel Folkestone has become a throughway for travellers to and from the Continent. So what does Folkestone have to offer?

It is not surprising that H. G. Wells and Charles Dickens found much inspiration in Folkestone. This elegant town with its picturesque old harbour and busy fishing fleet is truly delightful. Especially so, is the Leas Promenade. As you walk the mile along the promenade the cliff top lawns, a host of flower beds together with the panoramic views across the Channel to France are a pleasure to behold. This is the setting for the free Shepway Festival Airshow and also the Bandstand.

Just five miles from Folkestone, amidst charming countryside is Westhanger - the home for Kent's only racecourse. A new and spacious grandstand has been recently fitted, and there is ample parking. Westhanger

Station is conveniently located nearby.

Golf in Folkestone is very popular. The most established course in Folkestone is Littlestone which was used as a qualifier for the British Open. Two new courses have also been opened at Romney Warren and at Lydd where there is also a 20 bay floodlit driving range.

The coast from Dungeness to Folkestone and beyond the Goodwin Sands offers the best sea fishing in the U.K. and this is the venue for the European and All England Sea Angling Championships which are held annually. Freshwater anglers can enjoy the secluded lake in Brockhill Country Park near Hythe or along the leafy banks of the Royal Military Canal.

The flat terrain of Romney Marsh is ideal for a gentle stroll through the forests and country lanes and the undulating Warren situated in the famous White Cliffs is

Focus on Folkestone

perfect for ramblers. Cyclists can enjoy scenic lanes and the challenging off-road trails are ideal for mountain bikes.

Folkestone also has much to offer the would-be shopper. The sprawling seafront market is the South East's biggest, and is an Aladdin's cave for bargain hunters. Sandgate is a leading antiques centre, as is Hythe, with its charming Olde Worlde high street and shops.

Whilst in Folkestone you can visit the Rotunda amusement park. There are 17 types of rides and go-karting. It also has its own Sunday market which, with over 200 stalls, is an ideal place to find a bargain!

A relaxing walk along Folkestone Harbour will reward you with a regional variety of freshly caught seafood which will warm the cockles of your heart!

Leisure in Folkestone

Bandstand
The Leas, Folkestone. Military, brass & jazz band. Tel: 01303 253193.ext 321

Horse Racing, Folkestone Races
Westenhanger Racecourse, Stone St Westenhanger nr Hythe. Tel: 01342 835874,

Littlestone Golf Club
St Andrews Road, Littlestone, New Romney Tel: 01679 63355, 18 hole, 6,460 yard championship links course. Handicap required.

Lydd Golf Club & Driving Range
Romney Road, Lydd Tel: 01679 20808, 20-bay floodlit driving range. Open daily 10am-10pm. Also 18-hole, 6,700 yds links course.

Romney Warren Golf Course
St Andrews Road, Littlestone, New Romney Tel: 01797 362231, Pay & play.

Angling - Coarse
Brockhill Country Park, Saltwood, nr Hythe Tel: 01303 266327. Day tickets available on site.

Royal Military Canal
West Hythe Dam to Seabrook Tel: 01303 266334.

Angling - Sea
Folkestone Harbour (permit from tackle shops); Folkestone Warren; Rotunda Beach; Mermaid Point; Sandgate Riviera; Princes Parade; Seabrook & Hythe; Dungeness; Varne Bank & The Ridge (from boat) Charter boat bookings Tel: 01303 253881.

Tourist Information Centre
Harbour Street, Folkestone CT20 1QN Tel: 01303 258594.

Focus on Dover

Crossing the Channel from Dover to Calais is now traditional for the Brits.

So much so that we no longer notice the White Cliffs on our way out !

As you drive or even sail into the port of Dover, you cannot help but be overwhelmed by the towering stature of the celebrated White Cliffs - no wonder this area has been dubbed 'The White Cliffs Country'. If you venture above the White Cliffs to the east of Dover you will find yourself on The Langdon Cliffs which is part of the National Trust parkland. Here you can follow the cliff top trails and enjoy the stunning views across the Channel. On a clear day you can even see the French coast - some 21 miles away.

The Cliffs are also home to the famous Dover Castle, described as 'The Key of England'. You can visit the secret balcony high up inside the White Cliffs where Winston Churchill watched part of the Battle of Britain.

Close by you can see the Roman Lighthouse, which was built to serve as a guiding light for ships entering the harbour beneath. On the opposite side of Dover Castle are The Western Heights. Cattle lazily graze on these grassy slopes and in contrast with the more gentle scenery, these cliffs also have a myriad of fortifications, trenches and ramparts which were built in the 16th and 17th centuries. This area with its green slopes, delightful scenery, and many historical points of interest is perfect for cliff top exploration.

The area also has delightful countryside which abounds in beautiful scenery and wildlife waiting to be discovered. Frequent guided tours are organised by the White Cliffs Countryside Project, all year round, either by foot, bike or even by horse. These tours are generally accompanied by

Focus on Dover

an expert explanation of the countryside and its heritage.

One of the major attractions at Dover is the White Cliffs Experience. With the aid of films, re-creations and real you can see archaeological remains, you will discover historical Britain from the time of Julius Ceasar through to the Roman Conquest, Saxon and Viking Ages right up to the 1940s and World War II. Dover's own colourful history starting from prehistoric times, is also highlighted in the museum .

Turning one's attention to one of Dover's more relaxing venues; log fires, beer gardens and live music are all images that instantly spring to mind. Dover's traditional Kentish style pub culture is very popular and is an ideal way to enjoy an informal evening's entertainment perhaps with a pint or two with dinner.

Leisure in Dover

Dover Castle
Admission £5.50 children £2.80
Tel: (01304) 201268

The Western Heights
Access is from the Cowgate Steps

The White Cliffs Experience
Market Square, Dover
Tel: 01304 214566

White Cliffs Countryside Project
Guided cycle, horse rides and escorted walks & boat trips 6 Cambridge Terrace, Dover. Tel: 01304 241806

Cycle Hire, Dymchurch Cycle Shop
Tel: 01303 875296

Tourist Information Centre
Townall Street, Dover
Tel: 01304 205108

Pub of the Year Award winners:-
The Old Lantern Inn
Martin, off the Deal Dover Road nr Dover Tel: 01304 852 276.
Award winner 1991

The Crown Inn at Finglesham
The Street, Finglesham nr Deal Kent CT14 ONA Tel: 01304 612 555
Award winner 1992 & 1993

The St Crispin Inn
The Street, Worth nr Deal CT14 ODF
Tel: 01304 612081.
Award winner 1994

Out and About in France

A few essential tips to make your bargain-hunting travels a little easier ...
and perhaps a little cheaper.

En Route:
To comply with French motoring regulations, please note what is essential and what is no longer essential:
It is essential:
- To have a full UK driving licence and all motoring documents.
- To be over the age of 18 - even if you have passed your test in the UK.
- Not to exceed 90km/h in the first year after passing your test.
- To display a GB sticker.
- To carry a warning triangle.
- To wear rear seat belts if fitted.
- To affix headlamp diverters. These are widely available in motoring shops or you can DIY with black masking tape.

It is not a legal requirement to:
- Arrange a green card from your insurance company for France but check your level of insurance cover.
- Have yellow headlights.

Motorways & Roads:
French motorways (autoroutes) are distinguished by blue and white 'A' signs. Many motorways are privately owned and outside towns a toll charge **(péage)** is usually payable and can be very expensive. This can be paid by credit card (Visa Card, Eurocard, Mastercard) cash or even coins at automatic gates so be prepared. Contact an tourist board or information centre on the motorway network to find out the exact cost. Incidentally, the Calais to Boulogne motorway is toll free.

Other roads are as follows:
'D roads - routes départementales. These are generally the scenic alternatives to the 'A' roads.
C roads - routes communales.
Country roads.
'N Roads - routes nationales
Although toll free, these single lane roads are slower than 'A' roads.

IMPORTANT !
DRIVE ON THE RIGHT - OVERTAKE ON THE LEFT

Out and About in France

Breakdown on Motorways:
If you should be unlucky enough to breakdown on the motorway and you do not have breakdown cover, DON'T PANIC you can still get assistance.

The first thing you need to know is that there are emergency telephones stationed every mile and a half on the motorway. These are directly linked to the local Police Station. The Police will be able to automatically locate you and arrange for an approved repair service to come to your aid. Naturally there is a cost for this and fees are regulated. You can expect to pay around £50 for servicing plus the cost of any parts and around £55 for towing.
An extra 25% supplement is also charged if you break down between 6pm and 8am and any time on Saturdays, Sundays and national holidays!
At the garage, ensure you ask for un Ordre de Réparation (Repair Order) which you should sign. This specifies the exact nature of the repairs, how long it will take to repair your vehicle and, most importantly, the cost!

Emergency Phrases:

Please, help
Aidez-moi s'il vous plaît

My car has broken down
Ma voiture est en panne

I have run out of petrol
Je suis en panne d'essence

The engine is overheating
Le moteur surchauffe

There is a problem with the brakes
Il y a un problème de freins

I have a flat tyre
J'ai un pneu crevé

The battery is flat
La batterie est vide

There is a leak in the petrol tank/in the radiator
Il y a une fuite dans le réservoir d'essence/dans le radiateur

Can you send a mechanic/breakdown van?
Pouvez vous envoyer un mécanicien/une dépanneuse?

Can you tow me to a garage?
Pouvez-vous me remorquer jusqu'à un garage?

I have had an accident
J'ai eu un accident

The windscreen is shattered
Le pare-brise est cassé

Call an ambulance
Appelez une ambulance

Out and About in France

Speed Limits:
In France speed limits are shown in kilometres per hour **not** miles per hour. Always adhere to these speed limits as in France they are strictly enforce:

	MPH	km/h
Toll motorways	81	130
Dual Carriageways	69	110
Other Roads	55	90
Towns	31	50

When raining, these speed limits are reduced by 6mph on the roads and 12mph on the motorway. In fog, speed is restricted to 31mph As well as speed traps, it is useful to know that entrance and exit times through the toll booths can be checked on your toll ticket and may be used as evidence of speeding!

Roadside Messages:
For safety's sake, it is very important to be aware of the following roadside messages:

Carrefour	Carriageway
Déviation	Diversion
Priorité à droite	
	Give way to traffic on the right

Péage	Toll
Vous n'avez pas la priorité	Give way
Ralentir	Slow down
Rappel	Restriction continues
Sens unique	One way
Serrez à droite/ à gauche	Keep right/ left
Véhicules lents	Slow vehicles

Other messages:
Gravillons	Loose chippings
Chaussée Déformée	Uneven road & temporary surface
Nids de Poules	Potholes

Tyre Pressure:
It is crucial to ensure that your tyres are at the correct pressure to cater for heavy loads. Make sure you do not exceed the car's maximum carrying weight.

The following table gives a guide to how heavy typical loads are:

		Weight	
1 case of	Qty	kg	lbs
Wine	x 2	15kg	33lbs
Champagne	x12	22kg	48lbs
Beer 25cl	x 2	8kg	18lbs

Out and About in France

Parking For Less:

Illegal parking in France can be penalised by a fine, wheel clamping or vehicle removal. Since it is usually easy to park legally, (wherever you see a white dotted line, or if there are no markings at all) these penalties are easy to avoid. There are also numerous 'pay and display' parking meters which are generally very cheap. In Calais (not Boulogne), the good news is that these parking meters take English 10p, 20p & 50p coins. The French Franc coins they take are FF1, FF2 and FF5 which roughly equate to 11p, 22p & 55p making it slightly cheaper to use your English coins - *well, every little helps!*

Filling Up:

Petrol is a little dearer in France than in the UK, so fill up beforehand. Diesel prices tend to be similar.

To fill up, head for petrol stations attached to the hypermarkets (i.e. Auchan, Continent, PG Intermarché) as these offer the best value fuel. Though sterling is not accepted, credit cards usually are. Some petrol stations have automated payment facilities by credit card. These are generally indicated as 24 hour petrol stations and tend to be unmanned in the evening.

Petrol grades are:

Unleaded petrol - l'essence sans plomb.

Available in 95 and 98 grades - equates to UK premium and super grades respectively.

Leaded petrol - l'essence or Super

Graded as 90 octane (2 star), 93 octane (3 star) & 97 octane (4 star).

Diesel Fuel - gazole

LPG (liquefied petroleum gas) GPL

Drink Driving:

If you think that UK drink/drive laws are harsh at 80mg alcohol, think again! French law dictates that a 50g limit of alcohol is allowed. This equates to just 1 glass of wine. Exceeding this limit risks confiscation of your licence and an on-the-spot fine of anything between 200FF (£25) to 30,000FF (almost £4,000!)

Caught on the Hop!

Cafés generally allow you to use their toilets for free. Toilets in the shopping complexes may require a 1FF coin to gain entry If you see a white saucer, place a coin or two in it. In the streets you may come across the Sanisette, a white cylindrical shaped building. Insert 2FF in the slot to open the door. After use the Sanisette completely scrubs and polishes itself.

Out and About in France

Traffic News:
Tune in to Autoroute FM107.7 for French traffic information in English and French.

Phoning Home:
Phonecards (Télécartes) are widely used and available at travel centres, post offices, tobacconists and shops displaying the Télécarte sign. Coin operated payphones (becoming rare) take 1,2 & 5 FF coins. Cheap rate (50% extra time) is between 22.30hrs-08.00hrs Monday to Friday, 14.00hrs-08.00hrs Saturday, all day Sunday & public holidays. To make a call to the UK dial 00 Wait for the dialling tone then dial 44 followed by the phone number omitting 0 from the STD code.

Writing Home:
Post Offices (PTT) are open Monday to Friday during office hours and half day on Saturday. Stamps can also be purchased from tobacconists. The cost of a postcard home is FF2.80. The small but bright yellow post boxes are easy to spot.

Tourist Offices:
Known as Office du Tourisme - Syndicat d'initiative and are located as follows:
Calais Tourist Office is at 12 Boulevard Clemenceau opposite the train station
Tel: (00 33 3) 21 96 62 40

Boulogne Tourist Office is at Quai de la Poste
Tel: (00 33 3) 2131 68 38
They are closed Sundays lunch time (12.30-2.00pm)

Taxi!
It is cheaper to hail a taxi in the street or look for cab ranks indicated by the letter 'T' rather than order one by telephone. This is because a telephone requested taxi will charge for the time it takes to reach you. Taxi charges are regulated. The meter must show the minimum rate on departure and the total amount (tax included) on arrival. However, if the taxi driver agrees that you share the taxi ride, he has the right to turn the meter back to zero at each stop showing the minimum charge again. As in the UK, a tip (pourboire) is expected and it is customary to pay between 10-15%.

Currency:
French currency, known as the French Franc is abbreviated in 3 ways: FF or Fr or F. A Franc which is roughly equivalent to 11p is made up of 100 centimes. Centimes have their own set of coins (pièces) i.e. 5, 10, 20 and 50 centimes - marked as 1/2F. Francs come in the following coins 1, 2, 5, 10 and 20F and bank notes (billets) are in 20, 50, 100, 200 and 500F notes.

Out and About in France

Passports:
Before travelling to France ensure you have one of the following:
A full passport
A visitors passport s valid for 1 year
A British Excursion Document valid for 1 month.
These are available from main post offices in the UK.

Money Matters:
Changing money from Sterling to French Francs tends to be expensive. We recommend that you use your credit card as credit card companies give a better rate of exchange and do not charge commission when buying goods abroad. Of course you will require some cash. The most competitive place we could find to change money is in the port of Calais. There is a small 'hut-like' Bureau de Change offering a competitive rate of exchange without commission. Failing that, change your money in the UK where it can be a little more competitive than in France. You can also change money and cash travellers cheques at the Post Office (PTT), banks, stations and private bureaux de change. In the hypermarket complexes there are machines available to change your Sterling to French Francs. AVOID these as they are the most expensive method for changing money. It would be better to make a purchase in the hypermarket in Sterling, as change is given in French Francs without commission charges. Although convenient, be aware of the exchange rate.

Shopping by Credit Card:
To use your credit card ensure that you have your passport handy as you may be expected to produce

Shopping:
Supermarket trolleys (**les chariots**) require a (refundable) 10 franc piece. Keep one handy to avoid queuing for change.

Public Holidays:
Most French shops will be shut on the following days

Jan 1	New Year	Jour de l'an
Apr*	Easter Monday	Lundi de Pâques
May 1	Labour Day	Fête du Travail
May 8	Victory Day	Armistice1945
May*	Ascension	Ascension
May*	Whitsun	Lundi de Pentecôte
July 14	Bastille Day	Fête nationale
Aug 15	Assumption	Assomption
Nov 1	All Saints'	Toussaint
Nov 11	Armistice Day	Armistice1918
Dec 25	Christmas	Noël

*Dates change each year.

No Smoking!
The French have an etiquette for everything including smoking. It is forbidden to smoke in public places. There are quite often spaces reserved in cafés and restaurants for smokers!

Out and About in France

General Conversions:

What's Your Size?
When buying clothes in France, check the conversion tables below to find out your size:

Women's Shoes

GB		FR	GB		FR
3	=	35$\frac{1}{2}$	5$\frac{1}{2}$	=	39
3$\frac{1}{2}$	=	36	6	=	39$\frac{1}{2}$
4	=	37	6$\frac{1}{2}$	=	40
4$\frac{1}{2}$	=	37$\frac{1}{2}$	7	=	40$\frac{1}{2}$
5	=	38	8	=	41$\frac{1}{2}$

Women's Clothing

GB		FR	GB		FR
8	=	34	14	=	40
10	=	36	16	=	42
12	=	38	18	=	44

Men's Shirts

GB		FR	GB		FR
14$\frac{1}{2}$	=	37	16	=	41
15	=	38	16$\frac{1}{2}$	=	42
15$\frac{1}{2}$	=	39/40	17	=	43

Men's Suits

GB		FR	GB		FR
36	=	46	42	=	52
38	=	48	44	=	54
40	=	50	46	=	56

Men's Shoes

GB		FR	GB		FR
8	=	42	9$\frac{1}{2}$	=	44
8$\frac{1}{2}$	=	43	10$\frac{1}{2}$	=	45

What's The Time?

Central European Time (Greenwich Mean Time + 1 hour in winter and + 2 hours in Summer) is followed in France. This means that most of the time France is one hour ahead. The clocks are put forward 1 hour in the spring and put back 1 hour in the autumn.

Electricity:

If you wish to use any electrical appliances from the UK, you will need a Continental adapter plug (with round pins). The voltage in France is 220V similar to 240V in the UK.

Another important difference is that the French standard TV broadcast system is SECAM whereas in the UK it is PAL. This means that French video tapes cannot be played on English videos.

Weights and Measures:

Distance 1.6 km	=	1 mile
Weight 1 kg	=	2.20lbs
Liquid 4.54 litres	=	1 gallon
Liquid 1 litre	=	1.76 pints
Length 1m	=	39.37 inches
Area 1sq metre	=	1.196 sq yards

A Channel Shopper's Guide

Everyone knows that alcohol is cheaper to buy in France. But beware, not everything is a bargain! Included within these pages are the outlets we consider to be the best in Calais and Bolougne. We have also highlighted other information such as whether wine tasting (**dégustation**) is available, accepted payment methods, bus routes and, importantly, opening times. Some shops close for two hours during the day and some close all day Monday or Wednesday! Although there seems to be a lot of competition, closer inspection reveals that there are differences. Some outlets specialise in basement wines with a 'pile 'em high sell 'em cheap' policy, but offer very little in the way of service. Others are little more expensive but have a less frantic turnover of products allowing time for tasting and personal service.

To guide you we have included an appraisal of the outlet, plus where appropriate, a selected listing of products with a guide to prices so that you know before you go. An extensive wine listing for each outlet would be impossible due to the sheer variety (one outlet has over 1000 wines in stock!). However, it is extremely important to be aware that the more expensive the wine, the less the saving. This is because UK duty is influenced by the alcoholic content of the beverage. The rate of duty remains constant regardless of the quality or price range. Taking a bottle of wine that started life as a £1.00 bottle, a typical breakdown of its price once it has reached British shores is as follows:

Cost of wine	£1.00
Duty & VAT	£1.38
Shipping	£0.17
Retailer's Profit 30%	£0.76
Total cost	£3.31

The duty on a bottle of champagne is £1.50 and on a bottle of sherry is £1.40. An average saving of £1.50 on wine under £10 makes the purchase relatively cheap. More expensive wines attract higher percentages of profit leaving very little room for savings - if any! We have therefore confined our listing to wines priced at £2.50 or less where the reduction in duty makes a vital difference. Please note that prices are constantly fluctuating because of market forces and exchange rates. We aim to serve only as a guide and to steer you in the direction of your choice. All currency conversions shown are at a rate FF9.00 to £1.00 but check the prevailing exchange rate.

Calais Town

Calais is the closest French port to England and the evident touristic appeal centres around shopping. But is that all Calais has to offer?

Having suffered the ravages of war, Calais was completely rebuilt after World War II. Most people now see this port as a lattice-work of commercial streets, conveniently located solely to enjoy the benefits of cheaper shopping. Right?

Well, maybe not. Certainly its well established cross-Channel links and its geographical location makes it a good starting point to many destinations. The motorway network via the A26 and A16 means easy journeys to Strasbourg, Paris and Germany and, of course, the rest of France. Aside from its commercial centre, the Calais area also offers a good range of leisure activities. There are vast sandy beaches where you can enjoy activities such as sailing, sail boarding, speed sailing and sand yachting or just plain sun bathing. In the surrounding area you will find beautiful countryside where you can take a leisurely stroll or a ramble over the cliffs, in the woods and the hills. If you prefer more activity you can go off-road cycling, horse riding and even fishing. Escorted horse riding outings into the countryside are regularly available.

Along the Opal Coast, the dramatic landscape is forever changing. At the Cap Blanc-Nez you will find chalk cliffs, dunes and rocks. The high ground here affords some panoramic views across the Channel where, on a clear day you can see the English Coast. Further along the Opal Coast is the picturesque coastline of Cap Gris-Nez with its fishing villages. You can spend a delightful weekend just visiting the resorts and fishing ports. The area between the two Caps is known as 'le site des deux caps' and provides an attractive environment in which to spend a delightful weekend away.

There is also much to appeal to the nature lover. The Regional Nature Park, 'L'Audomarois' in St Omer, offers nature trails to explore the environment. It has been well preserved and the nature paths are well signposted. These trails can be made on foot, horseback or by bike. Guided tours are also available.

Golfing facilities around Calais are becoming ever more popular. If this is your sport then you will be pleased to know that there are three 18 hole golf courses nearby in Wimereux, St. Antoine and St. Omer.

And if all this is too much, you can always take one of the canal cruises along the waterways that criss-cross the Marais Audomarois and contemplate your next shopping trip!

Canal Cruises
Cruises with commentary which last 45-90 mins. Pont de la Guillotine, Rivage de Tilques (near St Omer). Call in advance Tel 21 95 10 19.

Cycle Hire
178 boulevard la Fayette.
Mountain bikes (VTTs) from FF100
Location VTT Brame Sports

Golf Golf du Bois de Ruminghem - 18 holes 1613 rue St-Antoine (20km south-east of Calais) off the N43.
Tel: 03 21 85 30 33.

Golf d'Aa-St. Omer
9 and 18 holes chemin des Bois, Acquin-Westbécourt Tel: 03 21 38 59 90.

Golf de Wimereux - 18 holes route d'Ambleteuse, Wimereux
Tel: 03 21 32 43 20.

Marais Audomarois
Fishing, rowing boats, boat trips & canal ('watergang') cruises Regional Nature Park Audomarois
Tel: 03 21 98 62 98
La Grange Nature de Claimarais
Tel: 03 21 95 23 40

Offshore Cruises
Sail down the Côte d'Opale on the yacht Ophelie to Cap Blanc-Nez
Tel: 03 21 93 63 71 or contact the tourist office.

Riding
For escorted countryside rides contact Cheval Loisir, 182 route de Gravelines, Calais Tel: 03 21 9718 18

General Market Days
Place de Crève coeur (map ref: D4/5) All day Thursday & Saturday a.m.

Calais Sights

Take in a few sights before returning home. After all Calais was under English rule for more than 200 years during the Occupation of 1347-1558.

Hôtel de Ville,
place du Soldat Inconnu

One of Calais' finest landmarks is the town hall which can be seen for miles around. This magnificent Flemish-style structure was completed in 1925 and dominates the main square. It houses many paintings and is adorned with stained glass windows. The interior is renowned for the elaborate decor of the reception rooms. Also attached to the town hall is an ornate brick clock tower.

Eglise Notre-Dame,
rue Notre Dame

It was here in 1921 that General de Gaulle married a local girl call Yvonne Vendroux. The architecture of this church is partly English Gothic in style, perhaps because it dates back to before and during the English occupation.

Les Six Bourgeois de Calais

The Town Hall. Inset : Rodin's Burghers

Citadelle
nr Square Vauban

This was originally built to house the town's garrison after the French retook Calais and dates back to 1560. In the 17th century much of the later work is attributable to the French engineer Vauban. These days it is partly used as a sports centre.

Musée de la Guerre
parc St. Pierre

The war museum is open daily from 10am-5pm from February to December. Entrance fee is FF15 (children FF10). This camouflaged bunker is situated opposite the town hall in an old German bunker. It served as a telephone exchange during the second World War. You approach it via a walk through the Parc St Pierre.

Musée de Beaux Arts et de la Dentelle, rue Richelieu.

This museum is open Wednesday to Monday from 10am to noon and 2pm to 5.30pm. Entrance fee is FF10 (children free).

It houses paintings from 15th to 20th centuries and sculpture from 19th & 20th centuries. Also on display are exhibits from Calais' lace industry - an industry originally brought to Calais from England.

Rodin's Six Burghers
place du Soldat Inconnu

At the foot of the clock tower and Town Hall stands Rodin's original 19th century bronze statue of The Burghers of Calais. The statue recalls the final year of the Hundred Years War when the mayor, together with other prominent citizens assembled here, wearing only their shirts, before surrendering to King Edward. They were willing to sacrifice their lives to save Calais from massacre at the hand of King Edward II at the end of his six month siege of the town. Their heroism moved the King's French wife, Philippine, to successfully plead for their pardon.

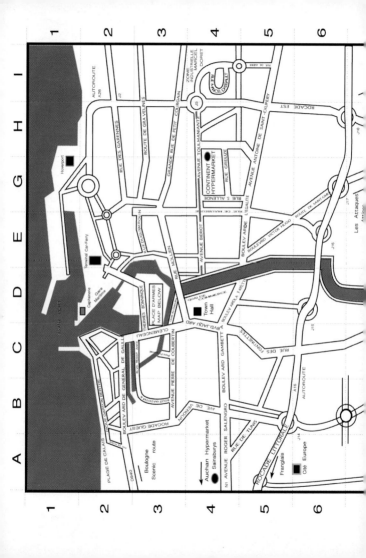

Aldi Supermarket
Rue Mollien
Calais

Map Ref:	E3
Bus No:	2
English:	No
Tasting:	No
Payment:	Cash only. Sterling accepted but the exchange rate is low.
Parking:	Yes
Open:	Mon-Sat 9am-7pm,
Closed:	Mon-Fri 12-2pm & Sun

How To Get There

From the ferry terminal follow signs to Centre Ville. At the roundabout take the second exit marked Centre Ville. Continue (railway on the left). At the end turn left into Rue Mollien. Aldi is 100 yards along on the right hand side in an inlet.

BEST VALUE BEER UNDER 15P PER 25CL BOTTLE MAÎTRE BRASSEUR BLONDE 4.7% ABV

On the surface, this looks like a very down market supermarket - and so it is.

Yet, among some outrageously bad wines there are one or two redeeming features.

The **Fitou** is very smooth under £1.50. The ripe currenty fruitiness of the **Côtes du Roussillon** makes it very quaffable and definitely a steal for £1.00. The sparkling **Crémant d'Alsace** at £2.70 goes down very well at dinner parties.

Stay away from the sparkling wine - Prince D'Aucourt at £0.81. Only buy this if you like the taste of thin sugared water. You have been warned!

Aldi also sell a great tasting pale ale which is ideal for parties: **Maître Brasseur Blonde 4.7%**. At just 15p per 25cl bottle this must merit some space in your car boot.

If you are shopping for a party, this is the best place to buy the crisps, nuts, olives and gherkins.

Aldi Supermarket

What's On Offer At Aldi?

Quantities 75cl unless otherwise shown. Prices in-store are in French Francs (FF) converted to Sterling (£) here for your convenience at a rate FF9.00 to £1.00.

Red wine less than £2.50	Origin	FF	£
Vin de Pays de L'Herault	France	4.95	0.55
Vin de Table Levendage	France	5.75	0.63
Côtes du Roussillon	France	7.95	0.88
Côtes du Rhône '93	France	9.95	1.10
Sangrilla Sol de Benidorm 1.5L	France	9.95	1.10
Côtes Belles	France	10.45	1.16
Fitou Rouge '92	France	10.95	1.22
Bordeaux AC '93	France	11.95	1.33
Bordeaux Supérieur	France	12.95	1.43
Vins de Bourgueil	France	14.95	1.66
Côtes de Bourg '93	France	14.95	1.66

White wine less than £2.50	Origin	FF	£
Blanc de Blanc Fruits de Mer	France	4.95	0.55
Bordeaux	France	6.95	0.77
Muscadet de Sèvre et Maine	France	11.15	1.24

Sparkling wine	Origin	FF	£
Crémant de Limoux	France	19.95	2.21
Crémant d'Alsace	France	21.95	2.43

Beer	% Vol	FF	£
Panaché (shandy) 10 x 25cl	-	10.95	1.21
Kusterbier 10 x 25cl	4.7	12.95	1.43
Ecu D'Or 6 x25cl	6.4	13.45	1.49
Special Upper 6 X 25cl	7.5	13.95	1.55
Brune Terken 6 x 25cl	6.7	14.95	1.66
Maître Brasseur Blonde 24 x 25cl	4.7	27.95	3.11

AUCHAN HYPERMARKET
Fort Nieulay, Route de Boulogne (RN1)

Map Ref:	A4
Bus No:	5
English:	Yes
Tasting:	Promotion wines only
Payment:	£, 💳 💳
Parking:	Yes
Open:	Monday to Saturday 8.30am-10pm
Closed:	Sunday

How to Get There

From the ferry terminal take the motorway following the signs for Boulogne and exit at Junction (sortie) 14 just follow signs for Coquelles or Auchan. From Le Shuttle cross the roundabout following signs for Calais and then follow signs for Coquelles or Auchan.

BEST CROSS-CHANNEL HYPERMARKET GROUP

Auchan Hypermarket was until recently known as Mammouth. The change of name has seen considerable improvements instore.

Generally the layout makes for convenient shopping, it is bright, colourful and spacious. The selection of wines come from all the major French regions with a nod here and there from Portugal, Morroco and Spain.

There is also an array of popular champagnes, beers and spirits which seem to be competitively priced.

Some good value wines on offer are the fresh lemony **Blanc de Blancs Spécial Fruits de Mer** at FF7.50 (83p) which at less than a £1.00 is a good cheap stand-in for Muscadet. The delicious mineral-edged **1995 Château Haut-Roque, Faugères** has a salty, savoury finish and worthwhile at FF22.50 (£2.50). The **1995 La Belle du Roy, Andéol Salavert** is simple, straightforward and good at FF45.95 (£5.10). Staying in this price range, try the **Chateauneuf du Pape 1995, P Chanau**, rich and meaty with a savoury aftertaste. Reasonable value at FF49.95 (£5.55). At FF16.30 (£1.81) you could try the **Bordeaux Blanc '96 P Chanau**, a simple wine with berry fruit on the palate. Auchan also have wine in a fruit juice style 1-litre carton, **Carré de Vigne Tetra Brik, Vin de Table de France** at FF8.40 (93p). Although a little thin it is palatable enough at the price. Another in this style is **Canterrane, Vin de Table Blanc**, FF5.95 (66p), not a great wine but surprisingly appealing, clean and fresh but good value at this price.

Watch out for 'promos' and see the 'Other Shopping Ideas' section for products which are at least 25% cheaper than in the UK.

What's On Offer At Auchan?

Quantities 75cl unless otherwise shown. Prices in-store are in French Francs (FF) converted to Sterling (£) here for your convenience at a rate FF9.00 to £1.00.

Red less than £2.50	Origin	FF	£
Vin de Pays de L'Aude	France	6.50	0.72
Pelure d'Oignon	France	7.95	0.88
Vin de Pays de L'Herault	France	7.95	0.88
Costray	France	8.15	0.91
Benoit Vin de Table	France	9.10	1.01
Corbières	France	10.50	1.17
Costières de Nîmes	France	10.50	1.17
Côtes du Rhône	France	10.95	1.22
Côtes du Roussillon	France	11.50	1.28
Merlot Vin de Pays d'Oc P Chanua	France	11.50	1.28
Côtes du Ventoux	France	11.95	1.33
Bordeaux Calvet	France	12.95	1.44
Côtes de Bourg	France	12.95	1.44
Côtes du Luberon Aigeubrun	France	13.50	1.50
Bordeaux Supérieur	France	14.50	1.61
Côtes de Duras Le Chevalier	France	14.95	1.66
Cahors de Clerac	France	14.95	1.66
Fitou	France	15.50	1.72

Auchan Hypermarket

Red less than £2.50 contd	Origin	FF	£
Medoc	France	16.50	1.83
Beaujolais Village	France	17.20	1.91
Cahors Carte Noire	France	17.50	1.94
Bourgogne Passe Tous Grain	France	17.50	1.94
Gamay de Touraine	France	17.95	1.99
Bourgogne	France	18.20	2.02
Cellier Des Dauphins Côtes du Rhône	France	18.20	2.02
Château Belles Rives Bordeaux	France	19.95	2.22
Malesan Bordeaux	France	20.20	2.24

White wine less than £2.50	Origin	FF	£
Hock Deutcher	Germany	9.95	1.11
Gros Plant Le Trotteur	France	11.95	1.33
Sauvignon Chanau	France	12.90	1.43
Sauvignon Chanau	France	12.90	1.43
Château la Foret Bordeaux	France	12.95	1.44
Entre 2 Mers Château la Tour Puymirant	France	12.95	1.44
Liebraumilch 1L	Germany	14.50	1.61
Sylvaner Strohl	Germany	14.95	1.66
Riesling Strohl	Germany	15.45	1.72
Touraine Sauvignon	France	15.50	1.73
Bulgarian Chardonnay	Bulgaria	16.60	1.84
Chardonnay Moillard Vin D'Oc	France	22.95	2.55

Rosé wine less than £2.50	Origin	FF	£
Rosé d'Anjou	France	9.95	1.11
Cinsault Chanau	France	10.95	1.17
Cantelune Vin de Pays	France	11.95	1.33
Côtes de Provence	France	11.95	1.33
Costière de Nîmes	France	13.95	1.55
Coteaux d'Aix en Provence	France	16.95	1.88
Viva Corsica Vin Corse	France	19.95	2.22

Sparkling wine	Origin	FF	£
Pol Remy	France	11.50	1.28
Muscabur	France	11.50	1.28
Rosabel	France	11.50	1.28
Paul Bur	France	16.10	1.79
Asti Spumante	France	19.95	2.22
Blanquette Cuvée Réserve	France	22.50	2.50

Auchan Hypermarket

Sparkling wine contd	Origin	FF	£
Volner	France	23.05	2.56
Saumur Cadre Noir	France	24.50	2.72
Crémant d'Alsace Keller	France	27.95	3.11
Clairette de Die	France	28.95	3.22
Saumur Ackerman	France	29.15	3.24
Blanquette Aimery	France	29.55	3.28

Champagne	Origin	FF	£
Amarande Brut	France	52.95	5.88
Veuve Emile	France	69.95	8.74
Nicolas Feuillate Premier Cru	France	79.90	8.88
Jacquard	France	84.15	9.35
Mercier	France	85.05	9.45
Canard Duchêne	France	89.40	9.93
Rothschild	France	86.75	10.84
La Demoiselle	France	105.00	11.67
Lanson	France	105.40	11.67
Lauren Perrier	France	114.50	12.72
Mumm Cordon Rouge	France	115.00	12.78
Taitinger	France	120.70	13.41
Moët et Chandon	France	125.25	13.92
Pomery	France	129.35	14.37

Beers	% Vol	FF	£
Panaché 10 x 25cl	-	12.50	1.39
Ch'ti 75cl	6.4	12.55	1.40
Carlsberg x 20	5.5	19.95	2.22
Tuborg 6 x25cl	5.6	19.95	2.22
Facon 24 x 25cl	4.9	29.95	3.33
Grölsch 24 x 50cl	5.0	117.00	13.00
Beck's 24 x 33cl	5.0	126.35	14.03
Carling Black Label 24 x 50cl	4.1	126.95	14.11
Newcastle Brown Ale 24 x 33cl	4.5	129.95	14.11
Old Speckled Hen 24 x 33cl	5.2	140.35	15.59

Carrefour Hypermarket

Carrefour Hypermarket
Cité Europe
Coquelles

Map Ref:	A6
Bus No:	7
English:	No
Tasting:	No
Payment:	£, Eurocheques, [cards]
Parking:	Yes
Open:	Monday to Friday 9am-10pm Saturday 8.30am-10pm
Closed:	Sunday

How To Get There

From Calais port turn left onto the A26. Follow the road signposted Dunkerque onto A16. Exit at junction (sortie) 18 following signs to Boulogne. Exit at junction (sortie) 12 signposted Cité Europe Ouest. Then follow signs to Cité de la Europe, Centre Commercial. You will soon see Cité Europe. Carrefour is on the right (or left depending on where you park) as you enter.

Carrefour is a giant hypermarket dominating the mouth of Cité Europe. It is brightly lit, well laid out, colourful and huge. So huge that some of the staff get around on roller skates!

The wines at Carrefour are stacked from floor to ceiling, yet the range is deceptively small. At less than £1 try the **Royal Marée** for FF7.60 (84p), a good cheap alternative to Muscadet, clean, crisp and lemony definitely a bargain! Try the **Gewurztraminer 1996 Cave Vinicole de Pfaffenheim**, lots of zippy lemon and apple FF29.80 (£3.08). A great Bordeaux example is the **1996 Baron de Lestac Entre Deux Mers** FF18.20 (£1.88), full of juicy gooseberry succulence. A smooth rosé to try is **Côtes de Provence Pierrefeu Domaines Fabre** FF15.45 (£1.60).

A very good red to try is the supple and tangy **1995 Minervois Domaine Le Cazal** FF16.50 (£1.75) - very good value. A stoney, fleshy **Château-neuf du Pape** is the **1994 Château de la Grande Gardiole** FF52 (£5.38).

Carrefour Hypermarket

There is an array of popular sparkling wines and a wide and varied range of beers together with a formidable range of spirits.

Their beers include a good range of Belgium Trappiste beers which are becoming ever more popular. The shelves also include a heavyweight from Germany - the EKU 28 - reputed to have the highest gravity of any bottom- fermenting beer in the world! Not a beer to be drunk by those with weak constitution.

What's On Offer At Carrefour?

Quantities 75cl unless otherwise shown. Prices in-store are in French Francs (FF) converted to Sterling (£) here for your convenience at a rate FF9.00 to £1.00.

Red wine less than £2.50	Origin	FF	£
Le P'tit Mousse Vin de Table	France	6.85	0.76
Courbières Rouge AOC	France	7.75	0.86
Minervois AOC	France	8.50	0.94
Le Catalan Rouge	France	9.90	1.10
J P Chenet Cabernet Syrah	France	13.70	1.52
Coteaux Lyonnais 1996	France	13.90	1.54
Costier de Nîmes	France	13.90	1.54
Cabernet Sauvignon	Bulgaria	13.95	1.55
Beaujolais	France	13.95	1.55
Merlot	France	14.50	1.61
Bourgogne Passe-Tout Grains	France	15.90	1.76
Anjou Rouge	France	15.95	1.77
Bordeaux 1995	France	16.90	1.87
Medoc 1996	France	17.00	1.88
Château La Chapelle 1995	France	17.05	1.89
Bordeaux Château Videau	France	17.95	1.99
Touraine Gamay	France	18.10	2.01
Saumur	France	18.30	2.03
Beaujolais 1996	France	18.80	2.08
Château Tour Camillac	France	19.00	2.11
Bordeaux Granjean 1996	France	19.50	2.16
Premier de Lichine 1996	France	19.75	2.19
Côtes du Rhône Villages	France	21.80	2.42
Côtes de Bourg	France	22.00	2.44
Bordeaux De Lestac 1995	France	22.50	2.50

Carrefour Hypermarket

White wine less than £2.50	Origin	FF	£
Castel Blanc Doux	France	8.55	0.95
Bordeaux Blanc Sec	France	9.00	1.00
Languedoc Lichet	France	11.35	1.26
Les Grappes D'or Sauvignon	France	13.50	1.50
Touraine Sauvignon Florian	France	13.50	1.50
Les Grappes D'or Chardonnay	France	14.30	1.58
Liebfraumilch 1996 1L	Germany	14.55	1.61
Anjou Blanc Hautiere	France	15.50	1.72
Coteaux de Languedoc 1996	France	15.80	1.75
Entre Deux Mers de Noange	France	15.95	1.77
Cankaya	Turkey	16.90	1.87
Muscadet Sèvre et Maine Sur Lie 1996	France	16.90	1.87
Gros Plan du Pays Nantais Sur Lie 1996	France	16.95	1.88
Bergerac Moel AOC	France	16.95	1.88
Riesling Vin d'Alsace	France	17.75	1.97
Sylvaner	France	18.80	2.08
Vouvray La Renardiere	France	19.25	2.13
Entre Deux Mers de Lestac	France	20.00	2.22

Rosé wine less than £2.50	Origin	FF	£
Vin de Pays du Var	France	7.80	0.86
Cinsault Rosé	France	9.90	1.10
Syrah Rosé	France	10.80	1.20
Le Catalan Rosé	France	11.05	1.22
Listel Gris	France	13.45	1.49
San Severo Rosato	Italy	13.55	1.50
Côtes de Provence	France	16.50	1.83
Sidi Brahim	Algiers	17.90	1.98
Bordeaux 1996	France	17.90	1.98

Sparkling wine	Origin	FF	£
Muscador	France	10.50	1.16
Pierre Vaubrun	France	14.2	1.58
Moscato Spumante	Italy	19.30	2.14
Opera Demi Sec	France	20.25	2.25
Charles Volner Brut & Demi Sec	France	22.25	2.47
Pol Aker	France	24.00	2.66
Crémant D'Alsace	France	25.05	2.78
Café de Paris	France	26.80	2.97
Asti Spumante	Italy	27.20	3.02
Clairette De Die	France	28.75	3.19
Ackerman Demi Sec	France	29.00	3.22
Aimery Blanquette de Limoux Demi Sec	France	29.00	3.22
Kriter Demi Sec	France	29.70	3.30
Cadre Noir Blanc Demi Sec	France	31.25	3.47
Saumur V. Amiot Demi Sec	France	32.00	3.55
Crémant de Bourgone 1992	France	34.45	3.82

Carrefour Hypermarket

Champagne	Origin	FF	£
Hubert DeClaminger	France	55.00	6.11
Raynal Brut	France	55.05	6.12
De Stall Demi Sec	France	73.80	8.20
Germain Demi Sec	France	74.60	8.28
Nicolas Feuillate	France	77.45	8.60
Alfred Rothschild Demi Sec	France	84.50	9.38
Mercier Brut	France	84.95	9.43
Mercier Brut Rosé	France	89.00	9.88
Canard Duchêne Demi Sec	France	89.50	9.94
Cazanove Rosé	France	95.90	10.65
Piper Heidsieck	France	106.00	11.77
Vranken Millesime	France	106.15	11.79
Lanson	France	112.00	12.44
Mumm Cordon Rouge	France	114.00	12.66
Pommery	France	119.60	13.28
Moët et Chandon Brut	France	122.50	13.61
Veuve Cliquot Ponsardin Brut	France	129.80	14.42

Beer	% Vol	FF	£
Bière d'été 6 x 25cl	5.0	16.80	1.86
George Killian's 6 x 25cl	6.5	19.50	2.16
Hoegaarden 6 x 25cl	5.0	20.85	2.31
La Becasse Geuze 6 x 25cl	5.3	22.20	2.46
La Becasse Cerise 6 x 25cl	5.0	22.85	2.53
Grain D'Orge 3 x 33cl	8.0	22.95	2.55
Leffe Blonde 6 x 25cl	6.6	24.35	2.70
La Bièr du Démon 3 xx	12.0	24.85	2.76
Bière Prestige Blonde Spéciale 12 x 245	6.1	25.30	2.81
1664 Brune 8 x 25cl	6.3	25.70	2.85
Ch'ti 6 x 25cl	6.4	26.00	2.88
Fosters Lager 4 x 50cl	5.0	26.70	2.96
Bud 6 x 33cl	5.0	27.80	3.08
Bière Sol 4 x 33cl	4.5	27.95	3.10
Spaten 6 x 25cl	6.5	28.25	3.13
EKU 3 x 33	11.0	29.90	3.32
Alsabrau 24 x 25cl	3.7	31.65	3.51
Guinness Export 3 x 33cl	8.0	32.40	3.60
Bière de St Omer 24 x 25cl	5.0	33.50	3.72
Artenbrau 24 x 25cl	5.0	33.95	3.77
Bière Blonde 24 x 25cl	4.6	35.10	3.90
Heineken 15 x 25cl	5.0	39.30	4.36
Semeuse 24 x 25cl	5.0	39.95	4.43
Kanterbrau 24 x 25cl	4.7	41.30	4.58
33 Export 24 x 25cl	4.8	44.05	4.89
Kronenbourg 26 x 25cl	4.7	51.35	5.70
Stella Artois 24 x 50cl	5.2	15.00	12.77
Caffrey's 24 x 44cl	4.8	149.00	16.55

Continent Hypermarket

Continent Hypermarket
Ave Georges Guyneme,
Calais

Map Ref: F4
Bus Nos: 2 & 4
English: No
Tasting: No
Payment: £, 💳 💳
Parking: Yes
Open: Monday to Saturday
            8.30am-9.30pm
Closed: Sunday

How To Get There

Exit the port at Calais and
turn left. Then follow the sign
for A26 autoroute.

After around 5 minutes take
exit at junction (sortie) 3.
Continue until you see signs
for Continent.

Continent hypermarket
dominates a large
shopping complex similar in
style to Auchan.

As you would expect it has a
huge range of products and
carries many 'promos' (special
offers). However, the
shopping experience here is
slightly dulled by the lack of
brightness and the dingy
decor.

You will however, find a
reasonable range of mostly
French wines including some
good Burgundies and
Bordeaux wines.

Try the **La Vielle Cure
Fronsac 1995** FF51.95
(£5.77) which is reasonable
value for a fully rounded wine
with earthy scents and soft
chocolate flavours.

There is usually a good
selection of competitively
priced champagnes alongside
a wide range of beers - one in
particular **La Bierre du
Demon** has a grand alocholic
content of 12%ABV!

Continent also have a good
range of spirits. See the Tipple
Table to see how their prices
compare.

Continent Hypermarket

What's On Offer At Continent?

Quantities 75cl unless otherwise shown. Prices in-sto
French Francs (FF) converted to Sterling (£) here for
convenience at a rate FF9.00 to £1.00.

Red wine less than £2.50	Origin	FF	£
Dmn Prieure de la Serre VDP L'Aude	France	4.95	0.55
Cahors Carte Noir	France	10.15	1.12
Côtes du Ventoux Hutchette	France	11.95	1.32
Côtes de Duras Château de Meneguerre '96	France	12.95	1.43
El Querba	Morocco	13.20	1.46
Bourgogne Passetout Grains Hutchette	France	15.90	1.76
Gamay Tourraine Hutchette	France	15.95	1.77
Beaujolais Hutchette	France	15.95	1.77
Côtes du Luberon Aiguebrun	France	15.95	1.77
Fortant Cabernet Sauvignon VDP D'Oc '95	France	16.00	1.78
Côtes du Marmandais 1994	France	6.20	1.80
Navarra Carta Rioja 1995	Spain	17.75	1.97
Cabardes Dmne Cros Vernède 1995	France	17.95	1.99
Fronton Villaudric Le Dispon	France	18.35	2.03
Beaujolais Villages Hutchette	France	18.45	2.05
Coteaux du Tricastin Haute Terres 1995	France	18.95	2.10
Coteaux du Tricastin Haute Terres 1995	France	18.95	2.10
Fitou Rocfamboyant 1995	France	19.50	2.16
Bordeaux Château Maurat 1995	France	19.85	2.20
Côtes du Rhône 1995	France	19.90	2.21
Santa Lucia Cabernet Sauvignon Mendoza	Argentina	19.95	2.22
Cabernet Sauvignon Bulgaria	Bulgaria	19.95	2.22
Côtes du Bourg 1990	France	21.95	2.43

White wine under £2.50	Origin	FF	£
Gros Plant Hutchette	France	9.95	1.10
Bergerac Blanc Sec Ecaille Mer	France	11.95	1.32
Sylvaner Strubbler 1996	France	12.90	1.43
Leibfraumilch 2Litre	Germany	14.95	1.66
Entre Deux Mers Ch. Bergey Montauran '95	France	15.95	1.77
Riesling Strubbler 1995	France	15.95	1.77
Niersteiner Gutes Domtal	Germany	16.95	1.88
Côtes du Rhône 1996	France	17.95	1.99
Gros Plant du Nantais La Perniere 1996	France	17.95	1.99
Muscadet Sèvre et Main Sur Lie	France	18.95	2.10
Soave	Italy	18.95	2.10
Chardonnay Vin de Pays de la France	France	19.95	2.21

Rosé wine under £2.50	Origin	FF	£
Les Béassières Vin de Table	France	9.95	1.10
La Stabella VDP du Var	France	10.50	1.16
Champlure Vin de Table	France	11.95	1.33
Fortant Grenach VDP D'Oc	France	12.15	
1.35Rosé Anjou	France	15.90	1.76
Côte de Provence Rosé Huchette	France	16.95	1.88
VDP D'c Fortant Syrah 1996	France	18.40	2.04
Côtes du Rhône 1996	France	18.90	2.10

Sparkling wine	Origin	FF	£
Muscat Roy Blanc	France	9.50	1.05
Muscat Roy Rosé	France	10.50	1.16
Courcelle Brut	France	14.90	1.65
Veuve Crezances Saumur Brut	France	20.50	2.27
Charles Volner Brut & Demi Sec	France	22.80	2.53
Jean Lafony Blanquette de Limoux Demi Sec	France	25.90	2.87
Blanc Foussy Touraine	France	25.90	2.87
Café de Paris Brut	France	26.80	2.97
Créman D'Alsace E. Duran Meyer	France	27.50	3.05
Ackerman Saumur	France	29.15	3.23
Kriter Brut & Demi Sec	France	29.75	3.30
Aimery Blanquette de Limoux	France	30.60	3.40
Crémant D'Alsace Dopff	France	34.95	3.88
Crémant de Loire Meyer	France	35.50	3.94
Gratien & Meyer Brut	France	35.95	3.99
Crémant Bourgogne Louise Bouflot Brut	France	36.95	4.10

Champagnes	Origin	FF	£
Keller Brut	France	69.90	7.76
Leonce D'Albe Brut	France	74.65	8.29
Germain Brut Reserve	France	74.90	8.32
Nicolas Feuillate	France	74.95	8.33
G H Martel Demi-Sec	France	79.90	8.87
Jacquart Brut	France	84.15	9.35
Canard Duchêne Brut	France	84.15	9.35
De Vallois Brut	France	84.90	9.43
Jean-Louise Mallard	France	84.95	9.44
Mercier Demi Sec	France	85.00	9.44
Mercier Brut	France	90.00	10.00
Cuvée Eugen Mercier	France	110.00	12.22
Laurent Perrier Brut	France	114.50	12.72
Taittinger Brut	France	120.75	13.41
Moët Chandon Brut	France	122.80	13.64
Pommery Brut	France	123.40	13.71
Veuve Cliquot Ponsardin Brut	France	129.80	14.42

Continent Hypermarket

Beers	% Vol	FF	£
Abbaye Triple Brune de St Landelin 33cl	8.0	4.95	0.55
Adelsheffen 50cl	8.8	5.50	0.61
EKU 50cl	4.9	5.50	0.61
Duvel 33cl	8.5	6.40	0.71
Chimay Bleu 33cl	9.0	7.10	0.78
Chimay Blanc 33cl	8.0	7.10	0.78
Leffe Radieuse 33cl	8.2	8.95	0.99
Jenlain 75cl	6.5	9.40	1.04
St Bernadus 33cl	10.0	9.95	1.10
Septante Cinq 75cl	7.5	10.20	1.13
Trappistes Rochefort 33cl	11.3	10.50	1.16
La Becasse 37.5cl	4.9	10.90	1.21
Ch'ti Blonde 75cl	6.4	14.45	1.60
L'Atrébate 75cl	6.0	16.10	1.78
Panache 10 x 25cl	-	17.25	1.94
Carlsberg 6 x 25cl	5.5	20.45	2.27
Kronenbourg 10 x 25cl	4.7	20.75	2.30
Lowenbrau Original 6 x 25cl	7.0	22.80	2.53
Bavaria 4 x 50cl	8.6	24.95	2.77
Budweiser 6 x 25cl	5.0	27.00	3.00
Koenigsbier 24 x 25cl	2.6	27.05	3.01
George Killian's 8 x 25cl	6.5	27.75	3.08
Koenisgbier 24 x 25cl	4.5	29.60	3.28
Fosters 4 x 50cl	5.0	29.65	3.29
Bruckbier 10 x 25cl	4.8	29.95	3.32
33 Export 24 x 25cl	4.8	31.10	3.45
Reine De Flanders 24 x 25cl	5.0	31.90	3.54
Orpal 3 x 75cl	5.5	32.90	3.65
1664 12 x 25cl	6.3	34.70	3.85
St Omer 24 x 25cl	5.0	34.95	3.88
Heineken 15 x 25cl	5.0	39.95	4.43
Seumeuse 24 x 25cl	5.0	39.95	4.43
Kanterbrau 30 x 25cl	4.7	42.80	4.75
Crest Export 24 x 25cl	4.8	109.20	12.13
Stella Artois 24 x 50cl	5.2	109.95	12.21
Grölsch 24 x 50cl	5.0	109.95	12.21
Badger Brewery 24 x 50cl	4.0	115.00	12.77
Amsterdam Navigator 24 x 50cl	10.0	115.20	12.80
Crest Super 24 x 50c	10.0	117.60	13.06
Mooreeke 14 x 70cl	5.0	129.75	14.41
9x Extra Strong 24 x 50cl	9.0	153.60	17.06
Holsten Pils 24 x 44cl	5.5	159.95	17.77
Caffreys 24 x 44cl	4.8	239.95	26.11

La Boutique Sainsbury's
Forty Nieulay, Route de
Boulogne (RN1)

Map Ref: A5
Bus No: 5 (take it from the
railway station)
English: Yes
Tasting: Promotion wines only
Payments: £, ▆▆ ●●
Parking: Yes
Open: Monday to Saturday
8.30am-9pm
Closed: Sunday

How To Get There

From the ferry terminal take
the motorway following the
signs for Boulogne and exit at
junction (sortie) 14 following
the signs to Coquelles.
From Le Shuttle cross the
roundabout following signs
for Calais and signs for
Coquelles.

**BEST CROSS CHANNEL
SUPERMARKET 1998**

**BEST VALUE CROSS
CHANNEL RED WINE 1998**
Sainsbury's Mendoza Cabernet
Sauvignon Malbec £1.82

**RUNNER UP BEST VALUE
CROSS CHANNEL RED
WINE**
Sainsbury's Jumilla £1.82

SPECIAL OFFER:
Spend over £20 and get
a **Free** bottle of the
award winning Best
Value Cross Channel
Red Wine 1998
*Mendoza Cabernet
Sauvignon Malbec*

Although Sainsbury's does
not have the largest
selection of wines in Calais,
probably due to lack of space,
they do have a variety of
consistently good wines. For
the second year running
Sainsbury's has won our Best
Value Cross Channel Red
Wine Award and this year has
won the Best Runner-Up
Best Value Red Wine Award
too.

The premises are much like
an off-licence and contain a
world-wide selection of
affordable wines especially
from the New World. Try the
award winning Chilean
Cabernet Sauvignon Malbec

Sainsbury's Supermarket

Mendoza at £1.82, a very dark wine with powerful plum flavours as well as sweet red grapes and red apples. Also from Chile is **Cabernet Sauvignon Maipo** at £2.18 which has a sweet edged currenty flavour and good balance. From South Africa try **Pinotage Western Cape** £2.29, a tangy wine with caramel flavours.

From the famous Burgundy area try **Macon-Chardonnay 1995 Domaine Les Ecuyers** at £4.49, honeyed aromas, full plump honey and melon chardonnay flavours with some Burgundian finesse. Another Chardonnay is the **Sainsbury's Chilean Chardonnay** which offers lots of tangy, zippy flavours at £2.47. **Sainsbury's Bordeaux** at £1.16 is simple and very good value for this clean, fresh, sappy, leafy wine. Another from Bordeaux is **1995 Château l'Ortolan, Bordeaux Blanc** and at £2.18, is a decent white with an Aussie Semillon style, chewy, fair and full. For an authentic Aussie wine, try **Sainsbury's Tarrawingee Grenach**, strawberry red in colour with a warm smell of blackberries, tangy taste and easy to drink. Good value at £2.59.

The Runner-Up Best Value Red Wine Award winner, the Spanish **Jumilla** is dark, sweet with chocolatey scents and chocolatey and plummy, oaky flavours - very good value at just £1.82. Another good value wine is the **Sainsbury's Portuguese Red Wine, Arruda** at £1.12 - appealing scents of dusty plums with lots of tannin and acid.

If it is bubbly you want try **Sainsbury's Blanc de Blanc Noirs Champagne** - £9.95 - earthy, rooty aromas with full apple flavours. There is also a range of familiar beers, many of which are not typically found elsewhere such as **Ruddles County** (saving £7.44 on 24 units on the UK price) and Webster's Bitter (saving a hefty £10.50 on 24 units on the UK price). Spirits tend to be Sainsbury's own with a choice of popular brands such as **Teachers** whisky 70cl at £9.88 (saving £1.81 on the UK price) and **Bells** whisky 70cl at £10.00 (saving £1.99). A bottle of **Pimms**, £9.29, will save you around £2.26 on the UK price.

Sainsbury's Supermarket

*Franc Galland,
Sainsbury's friendly
manager is shown here
dealing with an enquiry*

What's On Offer At Sainsbury's

Quantities 75cl unless otherwise indicated. Prices instore are in
French Francs and Sterling as quoted by Sainsbury's.

Red wine less than £2.50	Origin	FF	£
Sainsbury's Sicilian Red	Italy	9.90	1.16
Merlot Vin de Pays D'Oc	France	11.50	1.35
Sainsbury's Valencia Red	Spain	11.50	1.35
Bulgarian Cabernet Sauvignon/Merlot	Bulgaria	12.50	1.47
Cape Red	S Africa	13.50	1.59
Sainsbury's Sardinian Red	Italy	14.50	1.71
Sainsbury's Claret	France	17.50	2.06
Sainsbury's Bordeaux Rouge	France	18.00	2.12
Hardy's Banrock Red	Australia	19.50	2.29
Beaujolais Villages	France	21.00	2.47
Paul Masson Red	California	21.00	2.47

White wine less than £2.50	Origin	FF	£
Sainsbury's Hock	Germany	9.50	1.12
Liebfraumilch	Germany	11.40	1.34
Blanc Anjou	France	11.50	1.35
Blanc de Mer	France	12.50	1.47
Soave	Italy	12.50	1.47
Sainsbury's Sauvignon Blanc	France	13.00	1.53
Muscadet	France	14.00	1.65
Californian White	California	14.50	1.71
Chapel Hill Chardonnay	Hungary	15.50	1.53
Touraine Sauvignon	France	18.00	2.12
Rioja Blanco	Spain	18.00	2.12
Entre Deux Mers	France	19.50	2.29
Muscadet Sèvre et Maine Sur Lie	France	19.50	2.29
Gallo Chenin Blanc	S America	20.00	2.35

Sainsbury's Supermarket

Rosé wine less than £2.50	Origin	FF	£
Sainsbury's Sicilian Rosé	Italy	9.90	1.16
Portugese Rosé	Portugal	11.50	1.35
Rosé d'Anjou & Ardèche Grenache Rosé	France	12.50	1.47
Mateus Rosé	Portugal	18.50	2.18

Sparkling wine	Origin	FF	£
Sainsbury's Vin Mousseux	France	12.50	1.47
Asti-Spumante	Italy	19.50	2.29
Sainsbury's Australian Sparkling Wine	Australia	24.50	2.88
Sainsbury's Cava	Spain	26.50	3.12
Friexenet	Spain	37.00	4.35
Mumm Cuvée	California	57.50	6.76

Champagne	Origin	FF	£
Champagne Chaurey Brut	France	65.50	7.71
Sainsbury's Blanc de Noirs	France	84.50	9.94
Sainsbury's NV Champagne	France	89.50	10.53
Sainsbury's Rosé Champagne	France	89.50	10.53
Sainsbury's Vintage Champagne	France	99.00	11.65
Bollinger	France	182.00	21.41
Veuve Cliquot 1988	France	199.90	23.52

Beer	% Vol	FF	£
Bière d'Alsace 24 x 25cl	4.9	44.50	5.24
Burtons Draught 12 x 44cl	3.6	48.50	5.71
McEwans 12 x 44cl	4.5	49.50	5.82
Guinness Bitter 8 x 44cl	4.1	49.50	5.82
Fosters 12 x 44cl	4.0	59.00	7.00
Becks 12 x 33cl	5.0	59.50	7.00
Tartan 12 x 44cl	3.7	59.50	7.00
Guinness 8 x 44cl	4.3	59.50	7.00
Whitbread 24 x 44cl	3.3	64.50	7.59
Parkins Special 24 x 50cl	4.0	74.50	8.76
Heineken 24 x44cl	3.4	79.50	9.35
Blue Riband 24 x 50cl	4.0	79.50	9.35
John Smiths Draught 12 x 44cl	4.0	84.50	9.94
Tennet 24 x 50cl	4.0	89.50	10.53
Hofmeister 24 x 50cl	3.4	89.50	10.53
Stones 24 x 50cl	3.9	94.50	1.12
Sainsbury's Super Strength 24 x 50cl	8.5	99.50	11.71
Carling 24 x 50cl	4.1	104.50	12.29
John Smiths Bitter 24 x	4.0	114.50	13.47
Boddington 24 x 44cl	3.8	134.50	15.82
Tennents Super 24 x 50cl	9.0	144.50	17.00
Websters x 24	n/a	155.00	18.24
Carlsberg Special Brew x 24	9.0	168.00	19.76
Caffreys Irish Ale x 24	4.8	189.00	22.24

Tesco Supermarket

Tesco Vin Plus
Cité Europe
Coquelles

Map Ref:	A6
Bus No:	7
English:	Yes
Tasting:	Sporadically
Payment:	£, 💳 💰
Parking:	Yes
Open:	Monday-Saturday 9am-10pm
Closed:	Sunday

RUNNER UP BEST WHITE WINE AWARD
Chablis Premiere Cru Beauroy 1994 Cuvée Paul FF49

How To Get There

From the port turn left and continue onto the A26 motorway. Follow signs to Dunkerque onto the A16 motorway. Exit at Junction (sortie) 18 and follow signs to Boulogne. Exit at Junction (sortie) 12.
Then follow signs to Cité de la Europe, Centre Commercial until you get to Cité Europe. Tesco is on the lower level.

In true supermarket style Tesco is brightly lit and well laid out. They complement this with the very British 'car service' whereby you can obtain your purchases later from the collection point. This is definitely a blessing and a good alternative to carrying your shopping with you while you tour the rest of Cité Europe.

You will find a huge range of 1000 wines alongside many regional products. There is also a vast selection of beers including many Belgium beers such as Chimay Rouge and Bleue unfortunatley not listed here for lack of space.

Here are a few wines you may like to try: **Chardonnay-Chenin, Vin de Pays du Jardin de la France 1966** - FF10.90 (£1.21) - crisp, fresh and grapey with with some sweet creamy fullness of the chardonnay grape. The **Graves Yvon Mau** - FF17.90 (£1.98) offers very good value, it is clean, taut, oaky with a nice acid balance leaving a fresh zippy lemony aftertaste. Chile offers a very good value wine, the **1996 Caliterra Estate Chardonnay, Casablanca Valley** - FF28.50 (£3.16) - a tangy, citrus flavour with the Casablanca valley green leaf style. The **Tesco Chablis Premiére Cru** at FF49 (£5.44) is very good value, it is clean, fruit and bready, everything a Chablis should be.

The **1996 Bordeaux Rosé Yvecourt** - FF16.78 (£1.86) - has an orangey red rosé hue with light currenty fruit.

Another rosé to try is **La Rose Bayer 1995** -FF24.90 (£2.76) - lively with deep chocolate and current flavours.

The **Crémant de Bourgogne** - FF35 (£3.88) - is leafy, green, incisive and crisp. If claret is more your style, try the **Cuvée Aristide Saint Emilion** - FF49 (£5.44) - a soft, warm tangy ripe claret.

The **1990 Vina Mara Rioja Reserva** - FF28.50 (£3.16) - is a very good Rioja showing some age with softness, jammy, fullness and depth.

Great fun to drink is the **Tesco Australian Mataro, Murray Valley** - FF21.90 (£2.43) - strawberry scents, soft and fruity with pure red

What's On Offer At Tesco?

Quantities 75cl unless otherwise shown. Prices in-store are in French Francs (FF) converted to Sterling (£) here for your convenience at a rate FF9.00 to £1.00.

Red wine less than £2.50	Origin	FF	£
Roquefeuilles Vin de Pays de L'Aude	France	7.90	0.87
Tesco French Red Wine	France	7.90	0.87
Tesco Romanian Country Red	Romania	8.15	0.90
Tesco Minervois	France	9.90	1.10
Tesco Cabernet Sauvignon	France	9.90	1.10
Les Garrigues Côtes du Roussillon	France	10.50	1.16

Red wine less than £2.50 contd.	Origin	FF	£
Superplonk Red	Spain	12.50	1.38
Portico	Portugal	13.00	1.44
Tesco Beaujolais Nouveau	France	13.90	1.54
Tesco South African Cabernet Merlot	S Africa	13.90	1.54
Tesco Brazilian Cabernet/Merlot	Brazil	14.50	
1.61Château Les Comberies Bergerac	France	14.90	1.61
Château Barbe Bordeaux	France	14.90	1.61
Tesco Californian Red	California	15.50	1.72
Tesco Red Douro	Portugal	16.30	
1.81Celliers Des Dauphins Côtes du Rhône	France	16.80	1.86
Château Le Dragon Bordeaux	France	17.70	1.96
Le Piat D'Or	France	19.50	2.16
Tesco Vina Mara Rioja	Spain	21.00	2.33
Tesco Australian Grenache	Australia	21.00	2.33
Tesco Bulgarian Merlot Reserve	Bulgaria	21.70	2.41
Tesco Mexican Cabernet Sauvignon	Mexico	22.00	2.44
Tesco Canadian Red	Canada	22.00	2.44
Tesco Claret Superieur	France	22.50	2.50

White wine less than £2.50	Origin	FF	£
Stowells of Chelsea Chenin Blanc	n/a	7.00	0.78
Tesco French White	France	7.90	0.87
Fruits de Mer Vin de Table	France	8.50	0.94
Tesco Hock	Germany	8.50	0.94
Gros Plant VDQS	France	8.90	0.99
Muscadet Dmne Des Pecheurs	France	9.90	1.10
Chardonnay Chenin	France	9.90	1.10
Anjou Blanc	France	9.90	1.10
Tesco Bordeaux Blanc	France	9.95	1.11
Tesco Vin de Pays de l'Aude Blanc	France	9.95	1.11
Tesco Liebfraumilch	Germany	10.00	1.12
Tesco Reka Valley Hungarian Chardonnay	Hungary	11.50	1.27
Tesco Piesporter Michelsberg	Germany	12.00	1.33
Tesco Soave	Italy	12.50	1.38
Tesco South African White	S Africa	12.90	1.43
Tesco Corbières Blanc	France	13.75	1.52
Denbies English Table Wine	England	14.50	1.61
Tesco Australian Colombard/Chardonnay	Australia	14.90	1.65
Côtes du Rhône Blanc	France	16.25	1.80
Tesco White Graves	France	17.90	1.98

Tesco Supermarket

White wine less than £2.50 contd	Origin	FF	£
Edelzwicker	France	18.00	2.00
Tesco Baden Dry	Germany	18.00	2.00
Tesco Nuragus Sardinian White	Italy	18.30	2.03
Le Piat D'Or	France	19.50	2.16
Tesco Muscadet Sèvre et Maine Sur Lie	France	19.90	2.16
Nottage Hill Semillon	Australia	20.00	2.22
Alsace Pinot Blanc	France	21.30	2.36

Rosé wine less than £2.50	Origin	FF	£
Jean Duvignoble Vin de Table	France	8.65	0.96
Tesco Rosé d'Anjou	France	13.00	1.44
Mateus Rosé	Portugal	18.00	2.00
Tesco Bordeaux Rosé	France	19.30	2.14

Sparkling wine	Origin	FF	£
Pol Remy Brut/Demi Sec	France	7.50	0.83
Moscato Spumante	Italy	8.70	0.97
Veuve Aubin	France	14.90	1.65
Tesco Sparkling S African Sauvignon	S Africa	19.90	2.21
Clairette de Die	France	26.15	2.90
Tesco Blanquette de Limoux	France	28.00	3.11
Kriter Brut/Demi Sec/Rosé	France	29.00	3.22
E & J Gallo Brut Sparkling	California	29.90	3.22
Alsace Crémant Blanc de Blancs	France	30.55	3.39
Asti Spumante	Italy	34.60	3.84
Crémant de Bourgogne	France	35.50	3.94
Freixenet Cordon Negro	Spain	39.90	4.43

Champagne	Origin	FF	£
Canard Duchêne Demi-Sec	France	81.30	9.03
Tesco Blanc de Blancs	France	89.90	9.98
Piper Heidsieck Brut N & Demi Sec	France	100.00	11.11
Mercier Demi-Sec	France	114.00	12.66
Mumm Cordon Rouge	France	116.95	12.99
Pol Roger White Foil	France	142.30	15.81
Nicolas Feuillate	France	148.00	16.44
Veuve Clicquot Brut NV	France	149.00	16.55
Taittinger Brut Reserve	France	169.00	18.77
Dom Perignon Vintage	France	390.00	43.33

Tesco Supermarket

Beer	% Vol	FF	£
Winny 24 x 25cl	3.7	24.40	2.71
Gruber Bieres D'Alsace 24 x 25cl	4.5	27.45	3.05
Zorn Val 24 x 25cl	2.8	29.45	3.27
Magister 24 x 25cl	5.0	32.00	3.55
Tesco French Lager 24 x25cl	n/a	32.95	3.66
St Omer 24 x 25cl	5.0	35.95	3.99
Semeuse 24 x 25cl	5.0	39.00	4.33
Carlsberg Special Brew 4 x 44cl	9.0	39.00	4.33
Fischer La Strasbourgeoisie 20 x 25cl	4.9	39.60	4.40
33 Export 24 x 25cl	4.8	41.85	4.65
Bière D'Or De Flanders 24 x 25cl	n/a	42.00	4.66
Kestrel Lager 24 x 50cl	n/a	52.00	5.77
Kronenbourg 26 x 25cl	5.0	54.00	6.00
Tesco Best Bitter 24 x 44cl	n/a	57.00	6.33
Hofmeister Lager 24 x 50cl	3.4	60.00	6.66
Coors Extra Gold 24 x 44	5.0	69.00	7.66
Tennents Pilsner 25 x 50cl	3.4	69.00	7.66
Heineken Lager 24 x 44cl	3.4	70.00	7.77
Skol Lager 24 x 50cl	3.6	75.00	8.33
Castlemaine XXXX 25 x 50cl	4.0	82.35	9.15
Bishops Finger Strong Ale 12 x 5cl	5.4	89.00	9.88
Carling Black Label 24 x 50cl	4.1	89.00	9.88
Holsten Premium Bier 24 x 50cl	5.2	105.00	11.66
Kronenbourg 1664 24 x 50cl	5.0	105.00	11.66
Tennents Super 24 x 50cl	9.0	109.00	12.11
Tennents Extra 24 x 50cl	5.0	119.00	12.11
Grölsch Lager 24 x 50cl	5.0	129.00	14.33
Bass Traditional Draught Ale 24 x 44cl	4.4	133.20	14.80
Stella Artois 24 x 44cl	5.0	135.00	15.00
Holsten Pils 24 x 44cl	5.0	135.00	15.00
John Smiths Draught Bitter 24 x 44cl	4.0	139.00	15.44
Foster's Lager 24 x 44c	4.0	145.00	16.11
Fosters Export 24 x 44c	4.0	146.00	16.22
Boddingtons Draught Bitter 24 x 44cl	3.8	149.00	16.55

Beer Lovers Cash & Carry

Beer Lovers
Rue de Verdun 62100
Calais

Map Ref:	B4
Bus No:	4
English:	Yes
Tasting:	Not much
Payment:	£, 💳 💳
Parking:	Yes
Open:	24 hours
	Monday -Friday
	6am-10pm
	Saturday & Sunday

How To Get There
From the port take the St Omer Paris motorway for 2.3 miles, then turn off the Boulogne motorway (towards Boulogne) for 2/3 miles until exit (sortie) 14.
Turn right here and straight over the roundabout for 300 yards.
Beer Lovers is on the left.

Beer Lovers is a warehouse style cash and carry with many cheap and cheerful wines alongside some finer contemporary wines.

Some wines to try are **J P Chenét Réserve** a reasonable wine for £2.09 - The merlot nicely softens the cabernet sharpness yet its racy overtones still surprise.

You could try the juicy bugglegum style **Beaujolais Villages 1995** at £3.89 or the **Le Chambellan Moulin a Vente 1994 Henri de Villamont** - a smooth supple, decent wine at £4.49.

Also from Henri de Villamont is a delicious if slightly expensive **Mersault 1990**. An easy going, soft, meaty/spicey flavoured wine to try is the **Château de Paillet-Quancard 1994** at £3.99.

Very good value at £3.19 is the **Texas Cabernet Sauvingnon Ste Genevieve**, very smooth with a certain sweetness.

To add a little sparkle you could try the **Spanish Cava Hill** Sparkling wine which at £2.89 is a very soft honeyed flavoured quaffable bubbly.

Beer Lovers Cash & Carry

What's On Offer at Beer Lovers
Quantities 75cl unless otherwise indicated.
Prices instore are in Sterling.

Red wine less than £2.50	Origin	FF	£
Cabernet Sauvignon	France	-	1.09
J P Chenét Cabernet Sauvignon	France	-	1.59
Cépage Merlot	France	-	1.19

White wine less than £2.50	Origin	FF	£
Cépage Chardonnay	France	-	1.49
Cépage Cabernet Sauvignon	France	-	1.09
J P Chenét Cabernet Sauvignon	France	-	1.59
Muscadet	France	-	1.89
Cépage Sauvignon	France	-	1.19

Rosé wine less than £2.50	Origin	FF	£
Chapparrall Rosé	France	-	0.99

Beer	% Vol	FF	£
Gruber 10 x 25cl	4.5	-	1.70
Alsatia 24 x 25cl	5.2	-	3.59
Cruiser 24 x 25cl	5.0	-	3.69
Marten's 24 x 25cl	5.0	-	3.59
Stella Artois 24 x 25cl	5.2	-	5.69
Red Stripe 24 x 33cl	4.7	-	10.29
Becks 24 x 33cl	5.0	-	12.60
Fosters 24 x 50cl	4.0	-	12.69

Le Chai Ardrésien Cash & Carry

Le Chai Ardrésien
Route Nationale
Bois en Ardres 62610
Ardres

Map Ref:	Follow the road at G8
Bus No:	-
English:	Yes.
Tasting:	Yes, it is encouraged
Payment:	£, 💳 💳
Parking:	On the wide footpath outside or opposite.
Open:	10am-7pm 7 days a week
Closed:	-

How To Get There

From the Calais turn left onto the motorway, take the second exit and the immediate next exit onto RN43 (i.e Route de St Omer). On arriving at Ardres, midway to St Omer, Le Chais Ardrésien is on the left just past the first roundabout. From Boulogne, take the A16, come off at junction (sortie) 17 then follow the RN43 as per Calais.

Not strictly in Calais, this outlet, with over 1400 French wines representing all the areas of France, is well worth the 15 minutes detour. The husband and wife team of Paul and Bea Jones made their dream come true by establishing Le Chai Ardrésien in May 1993. Since then they have expanded and recently moved into this large and spacious outlet, complete with a 'dégustation' table. Here tasting on a generous selection of wines is available. For a serious tasting though, Paul and Bea welcome parties of 12 to 100

Le Chai Ardrésien Cash & Carry

people to enjoy their Le Chai Wine Experience. For £5.00 per head, they lay on a buffet and unlimited wine tasting. Salut! to an enjoyable and heady experience.

Paul Jones' own recommendation is the **Sauvignon St Bris** FF39 (£4.33), from Burgundy, the only appellation allowed to produce wine made from Sauvignon grapes. Paul describes it as slightly off-dry, full flavoured wine, which is good with fish.

Le Chai Ardrésien have also recently added 50 Kosher wines (which they intend to increase) to their selection.

The Jones' run a Members Wine Club. This entitles you to a 15% discount on all their products and invitations to wine tastings with buffets. Members also become eligible to join a unique system of investing in and receiving bonus wines.
To Join the club simply pop in with a passport photo or send it to them by post.

The large and spacious Le Chai Adrésien with wines from all regions of France.

Le Chais Cash & Carry

Le Chais
10 rue de Phalsbourg,
62100 Calais

Map Ref:	E3
Bus No:	2
English:	A little
Tasting:	Some
Payment:	£, 💳 💳
Parking:	Yes
Open:	9am-7pm daily
Closed:	12pm-2pm daily

How To Get There
On exiting the port turn right following the sign to Centre Ville. At the roundabout take the second exit.
At the end of the road turn right into rue Mollien. At the traffic lights turn right. Continue for 100 yards. Le Chais is on the right.

Le Chais is one of several branches dotted around France. There is outlet in Boulogne and also a small outlet in Cité Europe They specialise in French wine mainly from Bordeaux.

The range is complemented with a small selection of popular international wines such as the **Bellingham Shiraz Vintage 1986** FF24 (£2.62) from South Africa - leathery in style with soft flavours.

Another to try from closer to home is **Château Haut Maco**

Côtes du Bourg 1994, FF32 (£3.55), a light soft, currenty, easy going wine.

From the Rhône area of France try the **Côtes du Rhône 1996, E. Guigal** FF39 (£4.33), an intriguing, fat wine. Try also the **Macon Fuisse Jean Luc 1995** FF39 (£4.33), a soft, honeyed and lemony style wine with soft flavours of plum and chocolate - a gentle yet classy wine.

Le Chais also have a very wide range of Champagnes.

Le Chais Cash & Carry

What's On Offer At Le Chais?

Quantities 75cl unless otherwise shown. Prices in-store are in French Francs (FF) converted to Sterling (£) here for your convenience at a rate FF9.00 to £1.00.

Red wine less than £2.50	Origin	FF	£
Côtes du Ventoux	France	10.70	1.18
Cépage Cabernet Sauvignon/Merlot	France	13.50	1.50
Bordeaux Rouge	France	13.80	1.53
Côtes du Rhône Grandes Serres	France	15.00	1.66
Château Bel Air Bergerac 1992	France	17.90	1.98
La Galant Bordeaux 1994	France	18.00	2.00
Touraine Rouge 1995	France	18.80	2.10
Château Miot 1993	France	18.90	2.10
Cahors Côtes d'Olt 1994	France	19.80	2.20

White wine less than £2.50	Origin	FF	£
Blanc de Mer sec	France	11.50	1.27
Muscadet Sèvre et Maine	France	14.90	1.65
Touraine Blanc	France	17.90	1.98
Château Bel Air Bergerac Coux 1992	France	18.90	2.10
Château Launay Entre Deux Mers	France	19.80	2.20

Rosé wine less than £2.50	Origin	FF	£
Quercy Rosé	France	12.10	1.34
Langeudoc Rosé	France	12.90	1.43
Les Terrasses Rosé Ardêche	France	12.90	1.43
Syrah Rosé Ardêche	France	15.00	1.66
Rosé Anjou	France	16.40	1.82

Sparkling wine	Origin	FF	£
Mousseux Royal	France	9.90	1.10
Brummel Demi Sec & Brut	France	24.00	2.66
Vouvray Brut	France	29.80	3.31
Crémant de Loire	France	29.80	3.31
Saumur de Jessy	France	30.50	3.38
Bouvet Blanc de Blancs	France	38.50	4.27
Bouzy Rouge Lanson	France	105.0	11.66

Champagne	Origin	FF	£
Joseph Perrier Brut	France	96.80	10.75
Paillard Champagne Première Cuvée	France	99.80	11.08
Piper Heidsieck Brut	France	99.80	11.08
Lanson Demi-Sec	France	99.80	11.08
Lanson Brut Black Label	France	102.00	11.33
Laurent Perrier Brut	France	115.00	12.77
Taittinger Brut	France	118.00	13.11
Moët et Chandon Brut	France	125.00	13.88
Roederer Brut Premier	France	130.00	14.44
Veuve Cliquot Brut	France	135.00	15.00
Mumm Millesime	France	178.60	19.84

Eastenders Cash & Carry

Eastenders
14 rue Gustav Courbet,
Zone Marcel Doret

Map Ref:	H4
Bus No:	-
English:	Yes
Tasting:	No
Payment:	£, 💳 💳
Parking:	Yes
Open:	24 hours daily

**BEST VALUE SPARKLING
WINE**
Deinhard Lila Brut Riesling
£2.00

**BEST CROSS CHANNEL
SPARKLING WINE**
Seppelt Great Western Rosé,
£2.80

**BEST VALUE WHITE
WINE AT £1.50**
Wehlener Sonnenuhr 1994,
Wegeler Deinhard

**BEST VALUE CROSS-
CHANNEL CHAMPAGNE**
Champagne Millenium, £9.95

How To Get There

From the Calais ferry terminal turn left onto the A26 motorway and come off at the first junction you come to, junction (sortie) 3 following the sign to Z A Marcel Doret and continue to the roundabout where you will be able to see Eastenders.

From Boulogne follow directions to the A16 motorway to Calais. Come off at Junction 18 (sign posted Ports) and exit at junction (sortie) 3 following the sign to Z A Marcel Doret.

Eastenders was the first British Cross-Channel outlet in Calais. They specialise in providing the British punter with quality wine in the medium to cheap price range and Dave West, the owner, does so with gusto and without frills. At a recent visit, Andrea, one of our researchers, treated herself (hesitantly) to a very dusty and carelessly placed box of Beaujolais Villages at £2.50 a bottle. To her amazement she found her purchase to be extremely quaffable.

This warehouse style outlet is just that - dusty, chaotic but full of surprises. Their range of German wines seems to have triumphed at our wine tasting. Try the **Deinhard**

Eastenders Cash & Carry

Pinot Blanc 1993 Pfalz, £1.25 with rose scents and its soft and gently spicy flavours. Or perhaps the **Mission Peak Red** at £1.95, a dark, soft, salty, earthy fruity, Barossa Valley style wine but for half the price - good value wine. The Award Winning **Wehlener Sonnenuhr 1994, Wegeler Deinhard** at £1.50 is exceptional value - a classic mosel riesling and delicious summer sipping. Another highly recommended wine is the **Mosel-Saar-Ruwer 1990, Bernkasteler Graben, Reisling Spältese Trochen**, £1.50, a well aged, walnut/buttery bouquet, firm, dry, lingering apple flavours with a walnut finish. From Germany again try **Rudeshiemer Bery Rottland Reisling Kabinett** at £1.50, a richly dry, delicately, pear and greengage flavours. The **Deidsheimer Herrgotsader Reisling Trocken** at £2.00 offers dry apricot/peach aromas - a well balanced wine. Finally, we recommend the **Deinhard Pinot-Blanc Dry 1990 Rhenpfalz** - £1.25 - gently honeyed aromas and pear fruit flavours.

Unusual for Calais, is the range of kosher wines from around the world and from Israel. Try the White **Zinfandel, Samson 1993** - a rosé Israeli wine - which is a tasty mouthful at £4.95, or from the USA, the **Baron Herzog Chardonnay, 1993** at £5.50

To add a little sparkle to any party go for the aptly named **Lovely Bubbley** which at just £1.00, it certainly is. Or to add a little style, go for the award winning **Champagne Millennium**, full of sparkle and fruity, biscuit flavours which at £9.95 is undoubtedly the best mouthful of sparkle to be had at this price.

Eastenders have produced their own brand of beer - **ESP** - available in two strengths 5.2% and 9.2% both of which are great value at 17p and 23p respectively per 25cl bottle! What does ESP stand for? 'Extra Sex Please' said Dave West with a cheeky grin.

Eastenders Cash & Carry

What's On Offer At Eastenders?
Quantities 75cl unless otherwise shown.
Prices quoted in Sterling.

Red wine less than £2.50	Origin	FF	£
Bulgarian Cabernet, Novoselska Gamza	Bulgaria	-	1.00
Dry Red, Olympus 1992	Cyprus	-	1.00
Cabernet Sauvignon, Novoselska Gamza	Bulgaria	-	1.25
Merlot, Novoselska Gamza 1992	Bulgaria	-	1.25
Dom Mamede Vinho Regional Estremadura	Portugal	-	1.25
Moorook Dry	Australia	-	1.50
Cab./Syrah VDP de Gascogne J P Chenet '96	France	-	1.50
Valpolicella, Minini	Italy	-	1.75
Corbières, Château Maylandie, Maymil 1994	France	-	1.75
Mission Peak Red, Mendoza	Argentina	-	1.95
Merlot, Villa Rica, 1994	Chile	-	1.95
Malbec Mendoza 1992	Argentina	-	2.00
Cabernet Sauvignon/Shiraz, Captain Cook	Australia	-	2.00
Brouilly, Jean-Paul Sellès 1994	France	-	2.00
Merlot/Cabernet VDP d'Oc J P Chenet	France	-	2.00
Costillo los Molinos, Jumilla 1995	Spain	-	2.00
Cabernet Sauvignon Riviera, 1996	Australia	-	2.25
Bulls Red, 1995	Hungary	-	2.25

White wine less than £2.50	Origin	FF	£
Dry White, Olympus	Chile	-	1.00
Don Mamede, Vinho Regional Estremadura	Portugal	-	1.00
Bulgarian Chadonnay, Novoselska Gamza	Bulgaria	-	1.25
Sauvignon Blanc, Rodopski Roubin Ltd	Bulgaria	-	1.25
Côtes du Rhône, Celliers de Beauregard	France	-	1.50
Liebfraumilch, Liebling, Deinhard	Germany	-	1.50
Soave, Lovello, Cavigo 1996	Italy	-	1.50
Mission Peak, Mendoza	Argentina	-	1.75
Pinot Blanc, 1994	Hungary	-	1.80
Classic, James Cook	Australia	-	2.00
Semillon/Chard., Riverna, Captain Cook '96	Australia	-	2.00
Piemonte Chard.y, S Orsola 1995	Italy	-	2.00
Rioja, Juan de Acre	Spain	-	2.00
Côtes du Duras, Dm de Petitot, Hugh Ryman '92	France	-	2.00
Chenin Blanc K W V 1996	S Africa	-	2.20
Muscadet Sèvre et Main Dm du Perd son Pain '93	France	-	2.25
Apremont, Vin de Savoie, Dm Marc Vullien '93	France	-	2.50

Eastenders Cash & Carry

Rosé wine less than £2.50	Origin	FF	£
Griseley, Rémy Pannier, Erde	France	-	1.00
Rosé Valentin, Rémy Pannier, Erde	France	-	1.00
Côtes du Ventoux, Jean de Valdonne 1995	France	-	1.75
Beaujolais Planchon 1994	France	-	2.00
Cotes du Ventoux, Jean de Valdonne 1995	France	-	1.75

Sparkling wine	Origin	FF	£
Baron de l'Amour	France	-	1.00
Jean Dorsene, Brut & Demi Sec	France	-	1.00
Maquis de Calais, Brut & Demi Sec	France	-	1.00
Paul Rémy Brut & Demi Sec	France	-	1.00
Prince Henry Brut	France	-	1.00
Lambrusco Bianco, Donelli	Italy	-	1.00
Spumante, Burti	Italy	-	1.00
Regata Framboise	France	-	1.75
Moscato, Minini	Italy	-	2.00
Blanc de Blancs Brut & Demi Sec, Paul Bur	France	-	2.50
Veuve de Vernay Brut & Demi Sec	France	-	2.50
Seppelt Great Western Brut & Rosé	Australia	-	2.80
Novencento Ca'rubianco Dry & Sweet	Italy	-	3.00
Yalumba Angus Brut & Rosé	Australia	-	3.25
Killawara Brut & Rosé	Australia	-	3.75
Freixenet Cordon Negro	Spain	-	3.95
Carrington Extra Brut NV	Australia	-	4.50
Cuvée Napa Brut, Mumm	California	-	6.25

Champagne	Origin	FF	£
Champagne Raymond Henriot Brut	France	-	6.95
Champagne Saint Nicholas Demi-Sec	France	-	6.95
Champagne Millennium	France	-	9.95
Champagne de Nauroy Brut & Rosé	France	-	12.50
Moët et Chandon Brut & Demi-Sec	France	-	14.50

Beer	% Vol	FF	£
Uberland 24 x 25cl	4.5	-	3.50
ESP 24 x 25cl	5.2	-	4.00
Stella Artois special collectives 24 x 25cl	5.2	-	4.50
Wernesgüner 24 x 33cl	4.9	-	5.00
ESP 9.2 24 x 25cl	9.2	-	5.50
Lowenbrau Premium 12 x 28cl	5.2	-	5.50
Crest Export 24 x 50cl	4.8	-	8.00

Eastenders Cash & Carry

Beer contd	% Vol	FF	£
Oranjeboom 24 x 50cl	5.0	-	9.00
Carling Black Label 24 x 50cl	4.1	-	10.50
Becks 24 x 33cl	5.0	-	12.00
Budweiser Budwar 24 x 33cl	5.0	-	12.00
Badger Brewery - Dorset Best 24 x 50cl	4.0	-	12.50
Fosters 24 x 44cl	5.0	-	12.50
Grölsch - cans 24 x 50cl	5.0	-	12.50
Stella Artois cans 24 x 50cl	5.2	-	12.50
Two Dogs 24 x 33cl	4.0	-	12.50
Budweiser cans 24 x 33cl	5.0	-	13.00
Kestrel Super Strength 24 x 50cl	9.0	-	13.00
Skol Super Strength 24 x 50cl	9.2	-	13.00
John Smith's Bitter 24 x 44cl	4.0	-	13.50
Kronenbourg 1664 24 x 44cl	5.0	-	13.50
Strongbow Super 24 x 50cl	8.4	-	13.50
Guinness Original 24 x 44cl	4.3	-	14.00
Holsten Pils 24 x 33cl	5.5	-	14.00
Carlsberg Special Brew 24 x 44cl	9.0	-	15.00
Tennents Super 24 x 50cl	9.0	-	15.00
Caffreys Draught cans 24 x 44cl	4.8	-	17.00
Fosters Ice 24 x 33cl	5.0	-	17.00
Guinnes Original 24 x 44cl	4.1	-	17.00
Holsten Pils cans 24 x 50cl	5.5	-	17.00

The infamous Dave West outside his warehouse

Franglais Beer & Wine Cash & Carry

Franglais Beer & Wine
CD 215, 62185
Frethun

Map Ref:	A5
Bus No:	-
English:	Yes
Tasting:	Yes, extensive
Payment:	£, 💳 💳
Parking:	Yes
Open:	Daily 9am-7.00pm,
	Saturday 9am-6.30pm
Closed:	Sunday

SPECIAL OFFER:
A **free** bottle of red wine - Vin de Pays de Vaucluse 'Le Secret' - when you spend FF250 (around £27.00) on wine products but you'll need to show your Channel Hopper's Guide.

How To Get There
From Calais:
On exiting the port turn left onto A16-A26 motorway towards Paris-Reims. Continue to the autoroute to the A16 intersection. Take the A16 signposted Boulogne. Continue to exit (sortie) 11 signposted Gare TGV. Leave the autoroute and turn left over the bridge (D215). Franglais is 900 yards ahead on the right.

From Boulogne:
Take the A16 motorway towards Calais and then as above.

Franglais is bright with a relaxed atmosphere in which to shop. There are over 300 wines ranging from 84p upwards and eighty of these are available for tasting. Unique to Franglais is a state-of-the-art tasting room equipped with a Bar A Vin (wine bar) dispenser. This mechanism ensures that each wine is stored and dispensed into your tasting glass at exactly the right temperature. Gone are the days when wines for tasting were left open all day and ended up tasting of vinegar or something even worse! Franglais specialise in French wines. We suggest you try **Côtes du Rhône Le Meuieres 1996** - £2.32 - a light but very drinkable wine.

Another red is **Château Lacause 1996** - £2.86 - classy aromas with lively well balanced currenty fruit flavours or the **Château Meylandie Corbières 1994** - £2.85 - full of cinnamon spice and vivid, plummy fruit.

There are always 20 or so tempting special offers available. For example buy 12 bottles of **Muscadet Domaine de Beauregard** (single bottle price of £3.82) and get another six free reducing the unit price to £2.55.

What's On Offer At Franglais?
Quantities 75cl unless otherwise indicated.
Prices instore are in Sterling.

Red wine less than £2.50	Origin	FF	£
Cuvée des Molières	France	-	0.84
Cuvée de Patron	France	-	0.86
La Rachelle	France	-	0.95
La Mancha	France	-	0.95
Vin du Pays du Gard	France	-	0.95
Vin du Pays de L'Hérault	France	-	0.95
Vieux Moutier	France	-	1.07
Bordeaux	France	-	1.49
Bordeaux Château Haut Vallée 1996	France	-	2.06
Syrah	France	-	2.07
Costières de Nîmes	France	-	2.40
Côteaux de Languedoc Château de la Matte 1996	France	-	2.61
White wine less than £2.50	Origin	FF	£
Grappe d'or Blanc Moelleux	France	-	0.84
Blanc Sec Crustacés	France	-	0.87
Les Celliers du Bellay Blanc Dry/Medium Dry/Sweet	France	-	0.95
Entre Deux Mers	France	-	1.35
Comaine de Papolle Blanc 1995	France	-	1.50
Côtes de Bergerac	France	-	1.52
Côtes de Gascogne	France	-	1.98
Rosé wines less than £2.50	Origin	FF	£
Le Secret	France	-	1.36

Sparkling wines	Origin	FF	£
Doriant Brut or Demi-Sec	France	-	0.81
Baron de Rothberg Brut or Demi- Sec	France	-	0.91
Moscato Spumante	Italy	-	1.21
Grandial Muscat Blanc Doux	France	-	1.42
Chardonnay Blanc de Blanc Brut	France	-	2.04
Charles Roux Blanc de Blanc	France	-	3.06

Beers	Vol %	FF	£
Grölsch 25 x 25cl	5.0	-	6.63
Amsterdam Mariner 24 x 50cl	5.0	-	8.55
Bombardier 24 x 50cl	4.3	-	9.91
Stella Artois 24 x 50cl	5.2	-	10.89
Grölsch Dark Beer 24 x 50cl	5.0	-	11.18
Carling 24 x 50cl	4.1	-	11.46
Long Life 24 x 50cl	9.2	-	11.67
Tanglefoot 24 x 50cl	5.0	-	11.74
Crest 24 x 50cl	3.0	-	12.33
Holsten Pils x4 x 50cl	5.0	-	14.25
Bass 24 x 50cl	4.4	-	14.74
Fosters 24 x 50cl	5.0	-	15.98
Kilkenny 24 x 50cl	5.0	-	15.99
Caffreys 24 x 50cl	4.8	-	16.68
Fosters Ice	5.0	-	17.69
Draught Guinness 24 x 50cl	8.0	-	19.13

The state of the art Bar A Vins
at Franglais Beer and Wine

Inter caves Wine Merchant

Inter caves
26 rue Mollien
62100 Calais

Map Ref: D3
Bus No: 2
English: Yes
Tasting: Yes
Payment: £, 💳 💳
Parking: Outside
Open: Tuesday - Saturday
9.30am-12.30pm &
2.30-7.30pm Sunday
9.30am-12.30pm
Closed: Monday

How To Get There

From the ferry terminal follow signs to Centre Ville (second exit off the roundabout) Continue straight on (railway on the right).

At the end turn right into Rue Mollien. Inter caves is 200 yards along on the left hand side close to the traffic lights.

EXCLUSIVE SPECIAL OFFER:

on presentation of the Channel Hopper's Guide A magnum of Côtes du Ventoux Rouge cuvée prestige when you spend £75 or more.

Inter caves quaintly describe themselves as **'Les Chevaliers du Vins'** - the knights of wine! With 100 outlets around France, it seems a fairly accurate description.

This branch of Inter caves has a pleasant, cosy, non-rushed atmosphere. It is brightly lit and spaciously laid out. We are told that the wines are rigorously selected from hand picked individual growers and châteaux with an eye on quality.

This is a typical French outlet, with an exclusively French range with prices ranging from £2.00 to £20.00.

At £2.50 try the **Touraine Sauvignon De Neuville 1996** - fresh leafy scents and subtle flavours. An Even better value wine at its price is **Côtes du Marmandais 1993, Jean Marrens** at £3.50 - minty scents, silky super supple claret style flavours. Rising up the price ladder one more rung, you could try their **Vacqueyras 1995 Domaine Chamfort** at £4.60 - perfumed aromas, with soft, tangy ripe plum and chocolate flavours.

Inter caves also lay claim to being the leader in providing vacuumed packed bag-in-the box wines under the Réservavin label. Their selection of around 25 varieties come in 3, 10 and 20 litre tapped cartons which you are welcome to try before you buy.

What's On Offer At Intercaves?
Quantities 75cl unless otherwise shown. Prices in-store are in French Francs (FF) converted to Sterling (£) here for your convenience at a rate FF9.00 to £1.00.

Red wine boxes	Origin	FF	£
Vin de Table 10L	France	110.00	12.22
Cuvée du Chevalier 10L	France	125.80	13.97
Vin de Pays du Vaucluse 10L	France	145.50	16.17
Sélection Codivia (11%) 10L	France	149.50	16.11
Vin de Pays de la Drôme Merlot 10L	France	165.00	18.33
Prestige du Seigneur 10L	France	171.40	19.04
Sélection Codivia (12%) 10L	France	172.80	19.20
Vin de Pays de Côtes du Tarn Gamay 10L	France	175.00	19.44
Vin de Pays d'Oc Merlot 10L	France	178.00	19.78
Vin de Pays du Gard Cabernet 10L	France	179.80	19.98
Costières de Nîmes AOC 10L	France	197.00	21.89
Côtes du Lubéron 1992 AOC	France	197.50	21.94
Côtes du Ventoux AOC 10L	France	199.50	22.17
Bergerac AOC 10L	France	242.00	26.89
Côtes du Rhône AOC 10L	France	264.80	29.42
Bordeaux AOC 10L	France	279.80	31.08
Cuvée Fessy 20L	France	299.80	33.11
Côtes de Bourg AOC 10L	France	304.00	33.78
Graves AOC 10L	France	349.50	38.83

Intercaves Wine Merchant

Rosé wine boxes	Origin	FF	£
Vin de Pays Vaucluse 10L	France	155.00	17.22
Vin de Pays Gard 10L	France	181.00	20.11
Côtes du Ventoux AOC 10L	France	202.40	22.49

White wine boxes	Origin	FF	£
Vin de Pays Vaucluse 10L	France	155.00	17.22
Vin de Table 10L	France	159.80	17.67
Bergerac Blanc sec AOC 10L	France	200.30	22.26

Sparkling Wine 75cl bottles	Origin	FF	£
Vin Mousseux Brut Blanc de Blanc			
Veuve Arnaud	France	22.80	2.53
Crémant de Loire AC '87 Comtes de Loire	France	39.80	4.42
Crémant de Loire AC Maxim's	France	49.70	5.52
Saumur AC Cuvée Louis Francois	France	51.20	
5.69Crémant d'Alsace Blanc AC	France	51.80	5.75
Crémant d'Alsace Rosé AC	France	56.80	6.31

Champagne 75cl bottles	Origin	FF	£
Champagne brut De Saval Père & Fils	France	79.90	8.88
Champagne brut Carte d'Or J Estel	France	89.80	9.97
Champagne brut rosé Jaque Estel	France	98.00	10.89
Champagne 1ère cru Brut Azur			
Charles de Cazanove	France	106.00	11.78
Champagne brut Carte d'Or			
Prince Guy de Puyssat 1ère cru d'Ay	France	115.00	12.78
Champagne brut Cuvée de réserve			
Prince Guy de Puyssat Première cru d'Ay	France	116.80	12.98

Perardel Wine Merchant

Perardel
Rue Marcel Doret
Calais

Map Ref: H4
Bus No: 1 (closest)
English: A little
Tasting: Yes
Payment: £, 💳 💳
Parking: Yes
Open: 9am-7.30pm daily
Closed: -

How To Get There

Turn left out of Calais port onto the A26 motorway and exit at junction (sortie) 3. At the roundabout take the first exit signposted Zone Marcel Doret. Continue for a quarter of a mile until you see Perardel on the left hand side.

Perardel is an upmarket wine merchant with some cash & carry tendencies. The attractove premises are bright, spacious and a pleasure to peruse with wines neatly displayed on top of their boxes. There is an extensive fine wine selection with a few wines under £2.50. There are also some Liebfraumilch and wines of similar ilk but these seem a little out of place here.

The emphasis is on good .middle-range Burgundies, Clarets and white wines in FF25- FF65 (£2.77-£7.22) price range. Wines from Alsace and the Loire also feature to a lesser extent. Many French 'names' and vintages are on offer and there are many fine wines in the 'sell the silver' price bracket such as **Château Lafitte** for around £60.00 and **Château Latour** for around £55.00.

If you are tentative about wine, Perardel have a computer on hand which you can use to get a description of any wine that interests you. Alternatively fee free to experiment at the small but accommodating wine tasting bar.

Pidou Cash & Carry

Pidou

190 rue Marcel Dassault,
ZI Marcel Doret
Calais

Map Ref: H4
Bus No: 1 (closest)
English: Yes
Tasting: Yes
Payment: £, 💳 💳
Parking: Yes
Open: 24 hours

How To Get There

From the ferry terminal turn left onto the A26 motorway and exit at junction (sortie) 3 following the sign to ZA Marcel Doret. Take the first left, which initially looks like a caravan site, but slightly further on is Pidou.

Pidou appears to attract the bulk buyer, its large car park is continuously laden with trucks and coaches. Not surprising, since it has many attractive facilities such as a spacious car park, coffee machines, currency exchange and even a special check out for lorry drivers.

Shopping includes a souvenir shop, groceries and sandwiches. Outside there is a chippy -installed no doubt to make the British feel at home - and a hut like construction selling Belgian chocolates. Inside there is a wide selection of mainly French wines complemented by a range of international wines. Try the full flavoured, voluptuous **Paardendal Cabernet Sauvignon 1995** from Portugal which at £2.16 offers good value.

The shelves also have a good range of spirits (see the spirits comparison table) and a choice of beers large enough to entice any passing trucker! Pidou have another branch at ZAC des Pins, Transmarck (you can get there via A16 motorway taking junction (sortie) 19. The range here is similar and the shopping is less busy.

Pidou Cash & Carry

What's On Offer At Pidou?

Quantities 75cl unless otherwise shown. Prices in-store are in French Francs (FF) converted to Sterling (£) here for your convenience at a rate FF9.00 to £1.00.

Red wine less than £2.50	Origin	FF	£
Vin de Pays de L'Aude Adeline	France	8.20	0.91
Vin de Pays Bouches du Rhône	France	10.80	1.20
Corbières Sarmentier	France	11.50	1.27
Vin de Table Manerie	France	12.00	1.33
Cuvée du Patron	France	12.50	1.38
Bulgarian Country Wine	Bulgaria	13.15	1.46
Grand Dick	France	14.40	1.60
Bordeaux Rouge Carte D'Or	France	15.00	1.66
Minervois Cuvée Vigner AOC	France	15.90	1.76
Côtes du Rhône Chavaillon	France	16.70	1.85
Haut Medoc Lichine 1996	France	19.25	2.13
Rioja Tinto	Spain	21.40	2.37

White wine less than £2.50	Origin	FF	£
Vin Blanc Sec Festignere	France	7.70	0.85
Fruit de Mer	France	12.85	1.42
Bergerac Chanterelle	France	14.40	1.60
Vin de Pays Chardonnay	France	15.00	1.66
Liebfraumilch	Germany	15.20	1.68
Bordeaux Blanc Dazenac	France	15.30	1.70
Soave	Italy	16.55	1.83
Western Cellers	California	18.50	2.05
Sylvaner	France	18.75	2.08
Muscadet	France	19.10	2.12
Cabernet Sauvignon Paardendal 1995	S Africa	19.45	2.16

Rosé wines less than £2.50	Origin	FF	£
Rosé Sec Monchatour	France	11.20	1.24
Rosé Sec Manerie	France	13.90	1.54
Rosé d'Anjou	France	22.05	2.45

Sparkling wine	Origin	FF	£
Muscabur	France	14.90	1.65
Rosabel	France	14.90	1.65
Paul Bur Demi Sec & Brut	France	17.75	1.97
Liebfraumilch Sekt Sparkling	Germany	19.20	2.13
Pol Remy Demi Sec & Brut	France	23.35	2.59
Veuve de Vernay Brut	France	24.60	2.73

Pidou Cash & Carry

Sparkling wine	Origin	FF	£
Kraemer Blanc de Blancs Demi Sec Brut	France	28.50	3.16
Asti Spumante	Italy	30.85	3.42
Crèmant d'Alsace	France	35.00	3.88
Vouvray Bassereau Demi Sec	France	35.60	3.95
Volner Demi Sec & Brut	France	37.80	4.20
Kriter Brut de Brut	France	38.15	4.23
Crèmant Loire	France	41.40	4.60

Champagne	Origin	FF	£
Veuve Lorimet Brut	France	68.20	7.57
Dehours Brut & Demi Sec	France	79.15	8.79
Jacquart	France	89.50	9.94
Mercier Brut & Demi Sec	France	103.10	11.45
Castellane Brut	France	103.50	11.50
Mumm Cordon Rouge	France	121.35	13.48
Moët et Chandon Brut	France	139.35	15.48
Pommery Brut	France	143.25	15.91
Veuve Cliquot Brut	France	148.30	16.47

Beer	% Vol	FF	£
Bière du Demon 33cl	12.0	15.00	1.66
Brandeberg 24 x 25cl	2.8	27.95	3.10
Saerbrau 24 x 25cl	4.6	29.95	3.32
Bière Flasbourg 24 x 25cl	6.0	30.94	3.43
Bière Sembrau 24 x 25cl	7.0	30.95	3.43
Bière Blonde Lys 24 x 25cl	4.9	30.95	3.43
Bière Cruiser 24 x 25cl	4.9	30.95	3.43
Blonderbrau 24 x 25cl	4.6	32.95	3.66
Bière Magister 24 x 25cl	5.0	32.95	3.66
Bière Sphinx 24 x 25cl	5.0	33.95	3.77
Bière Kwik Pils 24 x 25cl	5.0	33.95	3.77
Bière Nordik Pils 24 x 25cl	5.0	33.95	3.77
Bière St Omer 24 x 25cl	5.0	33.95	3.77
Bière ASB	5.2	33.95	3.77
Bière Martens Pils 24 x 25cl	5.0	33.95	3.77
Burg Pils 24 x 25cl	3.0	34.95	3.88
Bière Sullington 24 x 25cl	6.2	36.95	4.10
Kanterbrau 24 x 25cl	4.7	43.90	4.87
Bière Millionieme 24 x 25cl	9.0	50.95	5.66
Stella Artois 24 x 25cl	5.2	52.05	5.78
Kronenbourg 26 x 25cl	4.7	53.80	5.97
Beck's Beer 24 x 33cl	5.0	124.60	13.84
Grôlsch 24 x 50cl	5.0	129.70	14.34
John Smith's Smooth 24 x 44cl	4.0	141.90	15.76

Victoria Wines Cash & Carry

Victoria Wines
Unit 139, Cité Europe,
62231 Coquelles

Map Ref: A6
Bus No: 7
English: Yes
Tasting: Not much
Payment: £, 💳 💳
Parking: Yes
Open: 10am to 8pm daily,
Friday   10am - 9pm,
             Saturday 10am-8pm
Closed: Monday

How To Get There
From the port turn left and continue onto the A26. Follow the road signposted Dunkerque onto the A16. Exit at Junction (Sortie) 18 and follow signs to Boulogne. Exit at Junction (Sortie) 12. Then follow signs to Cité Europe, Centre Commercial until you get to Cité Europe. Victoria Wine is on the lower level.

A cosy outlet, nestling in the lower level of at Cité Europe close to the restaurants , opposite MacDonalds.

Although the biggest selection of wine is from France, this is closely followed by wines from the New World. The rest are from Eastern Europe, Iberia, Italy and Germany.

Unfortunately there are no particular facilities for **dégustation** (wine tasting) outside of promotional wines, but the English speaking staff are highly trained wine buffs and offer the next best thing - helpful and knowledgeable advice about their wines.

There is generally a good range of wines on special offer amid the 400 varieties available. One fine example from Germany is **Slate Valley Dry Riesling** - at FF20 (£2.22) it offers an elegant floral nose, dry crisp and clean with green apple fruit.

Others to try are **Muscadet de Sèvre et Maine sur lie, Domaine de la Roulerie** FF24 (£2.60) (half the UK price), a pleasant, soft lemony example from the Loire.

If you like the taste of tropical fruits try the **Australian Deakin Estate Sauvignon Blanc 1996** at 26FF (£2.80).

Still on good form is Portugal's **AltaMesa Tinto Red** which at FF12 (£1.33) offers very good value for money. Victoria Wine also have range of spirits too. See the Tipple Table.

What's On Offer At Victoria Wine?
The following is a selection of what's in-store. Prices have been converted to £1 for your convenience.

Red wine less than £2.50	Origin	FF	£
Mendoza Red	Argentina	11.00	1.22
Vin de Pays de L'Herault	France	11.70	1.30
Côtes du Roussillon Red	France	13.00	1.44
Vin de Pays du Gard	France	13.50	1.50
Libertad Sangiovese/Malbec	Argentina	14.00	1.55
Bulgarian Cabernet Sauvignon	Bulgaria	14.00	1.55
Merlot/Gamza Suhindol	Bulgaria	14.00	1.55
Corbières Red	France	14.00	1.55
Merlot del Veneto	Italy	14.00	1.55
Firgrove Ruby	Chile	14.00	1.55
Cabernet/Cinsault Claret VW	France	15.20	1.69
Hungarian Cabernet Sauvignon	Hungary	16.00	1.78
Minervois Caves des Hautes	France	16.00	1.78
Fitou Mme Claude Parmentier	France	17.50	1.94
Côtes du Rhône	France	19.00	2.11
Big Franks Red	France	20.25	2.25
Le Piat D'Or Red	France	22.00	2.44
Château La Jalgue, Bordeaux Rouge	France	22.40	2.49
White wine less than £2.50	Origin	FF	£
Bordeaux Blanc	France	11.00	1.22
Le Midi Blanc VDP de L'Aude	France	11.00	1.22
Firgrove Chenin Colombard	Chile	11.00	1.22
Coba Falls Dry White	Chile	12.00	1.34
Russe Muskat & Ugni Blanc	E Europe	12.00	1.34

Victoria Wines Cash & Carry

White wine less than £2.50	Origin	FF	£
Liebfraumilch	Germany	12.00	1.34
Niersteiner Gutes Domtal VW	Germany	12.00	1.34
Altamesa White	Portugal	12.00	1.34
Nagyred Pinot Blanc	E Europe	12.75	1.42
Corbières White 1990	France	13.75	1.53
Hungarian Chardonnay Balaton	Hungary	14.00	1.55
Libertad Chenin Blanc	Argentina	14.00	1.55
Anjou Blanc	France	14.00	1.55
Slate Valley Country White	Germany	14.00	1.55
Esino Bianco	Italy	14.00	1.55
Muscadet Sèvre et Main	Frannce	15.00	1.66
Trebbiano Del Rubicone	Italy	16.00	1.78
Touraine Sauvignon	France	18.00	2.00
Big Franks White	France	20.25	2.25
Chenin Blanc KWV	S Africa	20.25	2.25
Cono Sur Gewürztraminer	Chile	21.00	2.33
Spaltese Bornheimer Adelberg	Germany	21.00	2.33

Rosé wine less than £2.50	Origin	FF	£
Portugeuse Rosé	Portugal	14.00	1.55

Sparkling wine	Origin	FF	£
Cava Coniusa Brut	Spain	13.25	1.47
Marquis de la Tour Brut & Demi Sec	France	15.00	1.67
Freixenet Cordon Negro	Spain	21.50	2.39
Great Western Brut Sparkling	Australia	26.00	2.88
Asti Spumante Martini	Italy	38.00	4.22
Mumm Cuvée Napa Brut	California	65.00	7.22

Champagne	Origin	FF	£
Mercier Brut Reserve NV & Demi-Sec NV	France	110.00	12.22
Lanson Black Label NV	France	150.00	16.67
Moët et Chandon NV	France	150.00	16.67
Veuve Clicquot Ponsardin DS NV	France	195.00	21.67
Champagne '89	France	200.00	22.22
Bollinger Grande Annee Brut '83	France	340.00	37.78

The Wine & Beer Company
Rue de Judee
ZA Marcel Doret
62100 Calais

Map Ref: H14
Bus No: 1 (closest)
English: Yes
Tasting: A Little
Payment: £, 💳 💳
Parking: Yes
Open: 8 am to 8 pm daily
Closed: -

How To Get There

From Calais follow the A26 motorway link road to the first Junction (sortie) 3. Turn left, signposted Z.A Marcel Doret (Journey time 3 minutes approximately) From Bolougne follow the motorway (A16) to Calais, and link road, signposted Car Ferry to Junction (sortie) 3. Turn right and follow signs to ZA Marcel Doret.

BEST CROSS CHANNEL SPARKLING WINE 1998
Seppelt Great Western Rosé £3.49

BEST CROSS CHANNEL ROSE WINE 1998
Château de Sours Bordeaux Rosé £5.49

The Wine and Beer Company is a British owned cash & carry and one of three in Calais. This branch is housed in a large warehouse style building, but without the usual chaos and dust generally associated with warehouse outlets. Wine & Beer offers a spacious, well laid out and a fun themed environment in which to shop.

The selection consists of around 400 wines from 16 countries offering a variety of styles. Though not the biggest selection in Calais, the beauty of this cash & carry is that if a wine tickles your palate, it will probably still be available on your next visit.

Chardonnay lovers have probably noticed the shift to unoaked styles recently. Wine & Beer have an example in the form of **Lindemans Conawarra 1996 Unoaked Chardonnay** £3.69 - it is fat, soft and you can taste some melon in its fruity flavours. From Burgundy try the clean, fresh sparkling wine **Crémant de Bourgogne Brut** at £4.99. A well priced red to try is **Merlot Vin de Pays des Coteaux de l'Ardèche** at £1.49 offers very good value for this chunky, chewy monster of a red. A good digestive would be **Château Signognac Cru Bourgeois Medoc 1992** £5.49 - drink up and enjoy. The **Château de Sours Bordeaux Rosé 1996** won the Best Cross Channel Rosé Award for its pleasing cherry pink colour, its balance and vividness and its pleasant fresh dry strawberry characteristics. The other award winner at this outlet is the **Seppelt Western Rosé Sparkling Wine**, a bubbley mix of strawberry scents and flavours, elegant and finely balanced.

Wine & Beer also have a selection of beers and a number of spirits and ports.

What's On Offer At The Wine & Beer Company

Quantities 75cl unless otherwise indicated.

In store prices are in Sterling

Red wine less than £2.50	Origin	FF	£
French Red	France	-	0.99
Vino Rosso and Lambrusco del Emilia	Italy	-	0.99
Merlot Gamza	Bulgaria	-	0.99
La Mancha, Table wine	Spain	-	0.99
Romanian Red	Romania	-	1.29
Merlot d'Oc	France	-	1.49
Cabernet Merlot d'Oc	France	-	1.69
Cape Red	S Africa	-	1.99
Bordeaux Rouge	France	-	1.99
Côtes du Rhône	France	-	1.99
Côtes du Roussillon	France	-	1.99
Coteaux de Tricastin, Dmne Brachet	France	-	1.99
Côtes du Rhône, Dmne Condamine	France	-	1.99
Bergerac Rouge	France	-	1.99
Corbières, Prieur Bubas	France	-	1.99
Minervois, Château Salauze	France	-	1.99
Costiers de Nîmes, Château Laval	France	-	1.99
Alta Mesa, Estremadura Red	Portugal	-	1.99
Fitou	France	-	2.29
Beaujolais	France	-	2.49
St Chinian, Domn Verdier 1995	France	-	2.49

White wine less than £2.50	Origin	FF	£
La Mancha Table wine	Spain	-	0.99
Millbrook, White English Table Wine	UK	-	0.99
Aligote Ugni Blanc	Bulgaria	-	0.99
Vino Bianco and Lambrusco del Emilia	Italy	-	0.99
Soldepenas, Valdepenas	Spain	-	1.49
Vino da Tavola Bianco	Italy	-	1.49
Moscato Spumante	Italy	-	1.49
Cape Chenin Blanc 1996	S Africa	-	1.49
Hock	Germany	-	1.49
Compte Tolosan	France	-	1.49
Leibfraumilch	Germany	-	1.69
Bergerac Blanc	France	-	1.69
Cape White	S Africa	-	1.99
Kumala Semillon Chardonnay	S Africa	-	1.99
Chardonnay Misket, Sliven	Bulgaria	-	1.99
Cabernet Melnik, Petritch	Bulgaria	-	1.99
Touraine Sauvignon	France	-	1.99
Soave Supériore	Italy	-	1.99
Muscadet Sèvre et Maine	France	-	1.99
Chardonnay d'Oc	France	-	1.99
Sauvignon Blanc, Ardèche	France	-	1.99

Wine & Beer Company Cash & Carry

White wine less than £2.50	Origin	FF	£
Lezeria, Ribatejo White	Portugal	-	1.99
Alta Mesa Estremadura White	Portugal	-	1.99
River Route Chardonnay, Matraalia	Hungary	-	2.29
Frascati Supériore	Italy	-	2.49

Sparkling wine	Origin	FF	£
Spumante, Frizzante del Italia	Italy	-	0.99
Vin Mousseaux, dry, medium and sweet	France	-	0.99
Moscato Spumante	Italy	-	1.49
Chardonnay Mousseux, Caves des Moines	France	-	2.99
Blanc de Blancs, Methode Traditionelle	France	-	3.49
Seppelts Great Western Brut & Rosé NV	Australia	-	3.49
Killawarra Brut NV	Australia	-	3.99
Asti Spuminti	Italy	-	3.99
Seaview Brut & Rosé NV	Australia	-	4.99
Saumur Brut Prestige, Methode Traditionelle	France	-	3.99
Salinger Brut 1991, Seppelt	Australia	-	6.99

Champagne	Origin	FF	£
Champagne Marie de Bissey Brut	France	-	8.99
Joseph Perrier Brut	France	-	12.99
Rochefoucauld Vintage 1988	France	-	12.99
Pol Roger Extra Cuvée, White Foil	France	-	14.99
Charles Heidsieck Brut	France	-	15.99
Lanson Black Label Brut and Demi Sec	France	-	16.99

Beer	% Vol	FF	£
Pilsor 24 x 25cl	4.0%	-	3.79
Cristalor 24 x 25cl	4.7%	-	3.99
Wendelbrau 24 x 25cl	5.3%	-	4.49
Stella Artois 24 x 25cl	5.2%	-	5.99
Ruddles Best Bitter 24 x 25cl	3.7%	-	5.99
John Bull Bitter 24 x 44cl	3.4%	-	8.99
Kronenbourg 1664 24 x 25cl	5.2%	-	9.99
Ruddles, Widget 24 x 44cl	3.7%	-	11.99
Becks 24 x 33cl	5.0%	-	12.99
Fosters 24 x 50cl	5.0%	-	12.99
Ruddles County 24 x 50cl	4.9%	-	12.99
Grölsch 24 x 50cl	5.0%	-	12.99
San Miguel 24 x 33cl	5.4%	-	13.99
Stein Lager 24 x 33cl	5.0%	-	13.99
Boddingtons 24 x 33cl	3.8%	-	13.99
Stella Artois 24 x 50cl	5.2%	-	13.99
Nastro Peroni 24 x 33cl	5.2%	-	14.99
Budweiser Budvar 24 x 33cl	5.0%	-	14.99
Kronenbourg 1664 24 x 50cl	5.2%	-	14.99
Draught Guinness 24 x 44cl	4.1%	-	18.99

Calais - Other Outlets

There are supermarkets and wine outlets galore dotted all over Calais. Below is a summary of some that have not received a full appraisal but are listed here for your information.

ALDI Supermarket
Ave du Verdun
Situated next door to Beer Lovers.
See their listing at Rue Molien.

CEDICO Supermarket
Rue Delaroche
Owned by Tesco. A bright supermarket - reasonable value shopping. Open on Sunday.

EDA Supermarket
Rue Mollien
Similar to Aldi Very dowdy.

INTERMARCHE Supermarket
56 Ave Antoine de St Exupéry
Many Vin de Pays wines available here and general shopping is also reasonable. Particularly useful to know that Intermarché have a petrol station offering cheaper petrol and it is open on Sunday.

MATCH Supermarket
• Bvd Lafayette
• 56 Place D'Armes
A stylish supermarket with a good Bordeaux selection and welcoming bakery.

PG Supermarket
• Ave Roger-Salengro
• Route St Omer
The locals shop here

PRISUNIC Supermarket
17 Bvd Jacquard
Highly visible due to its central location, but often more expensive

BWC Cash & Carry
63 Place d'Armes
Standard off licence with a range of popular products. It is situated on a busy tourist square and so prices tend to be higher.

BAR A VINS Wine Merchant
52 Place D'Armes
A quaint specialist wine shop which apparently doubles as a coffee bar but there are only two stools. The proprietor, Luc Gille, is anxious to press home the message that his stock of French wine is chosen by quality and not price - certainly no sign of Le Piat D'or anywhere! Products include French wines from Bordeaux, Burgundy, Beaujolais, Loire, Provence, Rhône, Alsace, Vin de Pays and of course, Champagne. Prices start at £2.50.

GRAND CRU MAGNUM Cash & Carry
24 rue de Commandant Bonningu
A specialist wine warehouse with most Bordeaux wines.

ROYAL CHAMPAGNE Specialist
9 rue André Gerschell Tiny champagne specialist with a small selection of vintage champagnes

LE TERROIR Wine Merchant
29 rue des Fontinettes
Small, pleasant outlet with a specialist selection of vintage and hard to find wines.

What is Cité Europe?

With representation from every European country, you instantly become an international shopper just by walking through the doors of Cité Europe!

Cité Europe is grandly located in the village of Coquelles in Calais, an area that just a few years ago - prior to the development of Eurotunnel and Cité Europe - was simply a main village road.

The name Coquelles is thought to be of Latin origin. The first Lords of Coquelles are mentioned in 1183 with Eustache de Kalquella when the village was situated near the old tower remains of the 13th century church of Old Coquelles.

At that time it was just a small hamlet and since then it has had a series of European occupants:
- the Romans, the English for over two centuries, the Spanish for a mere two years and the Germans for four years.

How apt that Cité Europe should be built on this very European site.

The philosophy behind Cité Europe is to bring to the shopper a truly cosmopolitan choice of shops. Each European country is represented in this immense indoor shopping centre.

Some 59,000 square metres on two levels is home to 11 major stores, including a hypermarket and 150 shops selling everything you can imagine from all over Europe. Familiar names are The Body Shop, Etam, Tesco, Tie Rack and Toys R Us.

What is Cité Europe?

The myriad of restaurants are just as diverse, offering everything from Sauerkraut to pizzas and hamburgers from the omnipresent MacDonalds. There's even a pub where you can enjoy a pint or two.

Some parts of the dining area are built in the style of the respective country designed to enhance the international flavour and ambience.

Leisure is also considered an important aspect of Cité Europe. With this in mind Cité Europe also has a12 screen cinema complex to accommodate all viewing preferences.

For the kids there is an adventure playground, a merry-go-round, simulators and a variety of video games.

And finally, not forgetting the wine, beers and spirits, you can enjoy a wonderful shopping day out and still go home with alcoholic bargains from Carrefour Hypermarket, Tesco Supermarket, Victoria Wines or Le Chais.cash and carries.

How To Get There

Cité Europe is situated opposite Eurotunnel Ideal for those travelling with Le Shuttle

From Calais port , turn left as you come out and join the A26 Autoroute. Then join the A16 Autoroute following signs to Boulogne exiting at Junction 12 (sortie 12).

Bus Route No: 7

Calais Map Ref: A6

DAY TRIPPERS BEWARE!
A visit to Cité Europe
is a day trip in itself
once there you will find
it very difficult to leave.

D940 - The Scenic Route

*D940, N1, A16 -
These are not codes,
but 3 different routes
from Calais to
Bolougne. So which one
do you take?*

Initially, the N1 was
considered the main
link between Calais
and Boulogne.
However this was
superseded by the
A16 motorway,
enabling a 20 minute
dash between the two
towns. Parallel to the
A16 and N1 is one of
the area's best kept
secrets - **the D940**.

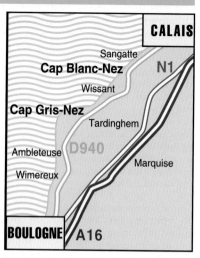

This is the scenic coastal
route which ambles lazily
along the Côte d'Opale. It
will get you to Boulogne...
eventually. Pick it up by the
Calais plage (beach)
signposted Boulogne par la
Côte and head in the
direction of Sangatte.

This long and winding road
takes you through Bleriot
Plage and over to the
undulating chalk hills of Cap
Blanc Nez and Cap Gris Nez.
Take time-out here and make
your way to their zeniths for a

great visual rhapsody of
untamed cliffs, the rugged
greenery, the blue of the sky
all reflected in the expanse of
the sea.

Sandwiched between these
headlands are the tiny fishing
villages of Escalles and
Wissant.

In Escalles there's a panoramic
dining opportunity at a
restaurant called Le Thomé
de Gamond perched humbly
on the top of Mont Hubert. If
you dine here make sure you

get a table by the large windows. Next door is the Musée de Transmanche, a museum about cross-Channel transport.

At Wissant you can see the fishermen selling their wares almost straight from the sea. Their fishing boats containing the catch of the day are hauled into the village square and they trade direct from their boats.

In fact, dotted all along the D940 route are many temptations to lure you to stop and shop. You may see farmers selling their freshly grown fruit and vegetables in open huts. These are usually located by the roadside. Or you may see signs directing you to places where you can buy fresh seafood or even flowers.

Further along, the D940 are the quaint villages of Ambleteuse and Ardinghem Both these villages are culturally noteworthy as each has its own War Museum both of which are worth visting before arriving in Wimereux.

Situated at the foot of Boulogne- just six miles away is Wimereux - a beautiful picture postcard seaside resort. Its sandy beaches makes Wimereux popular with the French and foreign tourists alike. As well as the promenade and beach there are pretty streets with quaint cafés and shops.

Wimereux is also home to **Mille Vignes** wine merchant, the winner of The Channel Hopper's Guide Best Cross Channel Wine Outlet of the year Award.

A few sand dunes later, the D940 finally ends and Boulogne begins....

Boulogne Beach

Legend has it that in 636 AD a boat carrying only a statue of the Virgin Mary washed up on the beach of Boulogne and made it a pilgrimage site. Now they gather for the fish !

Boulogne is considered a very pleasant stopover for thousands of travellers, but those staying a little longer can enjoy the beauty, charm and heritage of this town. The town itself is laced with quaint streets and shops and if you walk past the tidal harbour as far as the beach to the Sailor's Calvalry you will be rewarded with a good view of the port.

If you venture higher up to the old city (vieille ville) you will find the 13th century ramparts - miraculously unscathed after World War II. They surround a network of narrow cobbled streets where you can find peace from the madding crowds and enjoy a peaceful and romantic walk. Boulogne's claim to fame is that it is France's premier fishing port - in fact a quarter

of Boulogne's population are involved in fishing. Every year Boulogne celebrates its Fête du Poisson (Fish Festival) during July 12-18 when 20,000 fish and seafood enthusiasts come to enjoy the grand procession led in spirit by the Virign Mary in her capacity as Patron saint of fishermen.

A major attraction is the Nausicaa national sea centre. It is only a few moments from the port with its own restaurant and multi-media library. At Nausicaa you can enjoy the wonders of the underwater world and experience the interactive terminals to the underwater observation tanks including the shark aquarium. In case all that marine watching makes you hungry, Nausicaa also has two restaurants offering anything from a sandwich to a 3 course meal. Boulogne has its own nature reserve at the Parc Naturel Regional 'Boulonnais'. The area from the bay of Authie to the Oye beach, some 100km of coast line, is adorned with cliffs, dunes and marshes, and is preserved as a safe haven for birds and plants. Footpaths have been created for visitors and guided tours are organised to discover the national heritage.

Boulogne has its own forest spanning over 200 hectares. You can enjoy a hearty ramble through the 13 kilometres of signposted footpaths or if you prefer more exhileration, try cross-country horse riding. Alternatively you can hire a bicycle for a leisurely pedal through the countryside.

Golfers can tee off at no less than three 18 hole golf courses; one at Wimereux and two in Hardelot.

Perhaps, a little shopping at one of the hypermarkets followed by a relaxing drink and croissant is more your style. If so, you will be pleased with the myriad of restaurants and continental style cafés Boulogne has to offer.

Leisure in Boulogne
Nausicaa Centre National de la Mer Boulevard Sainte-Beuve Open daily - 10am-6pm. Located just minutes from Seacat.
Tel: 03 21 30 99 99

Parc naturel régional du Boulonnais Maison du Parc à le Wast
Tel: (00 33) 3 21 83 38 79

Golf - (all 18 holes)
Golf de Wimereux, route d'Ambleteuse, Wimereux
Tel: (00 33) 3 21 32 43 20
Golf des Pins
avenue de Golf, Hardelot
Tel: (00 33) 3 21 83 73 10
Golf des Dunes
avenue Edouard VII Hardelot
Tel: (00 33) 3 21 91 90 90

Horse Riding Centre Équestre du Boulonnais
Tel: (00 33) 3 21 83 32 38

Bicycle Hire
Youth Hotel, Rue Porte Gayole
Tel: (00 33) 3 21 83 32 59

Fish Market
Quai Gambetta Mon. to Sat. mornings. Opposite SeaCat Port.

General Market Days
Place Dalton. All day Wed & Sat

Sea Fishing
Fishing Club Boulonnais, 3 rue Coquelin, Boulogne
Tel: 03 21 87 55 99

Boulogne Sights

Touristic brochures applaud the charm and beauty of Boulogne, but is it just a pretty face?

Hôtel de Ville,
Place de la Résistance

The town hall has been altered six times since it was restored in the 18th century. It houses oil portrait paintings and the Wedding Room contains wood carvings from Dutch Oak.

Château-Museé
rue de Bernet

There is so much to see in this mediaeval Château Museum you may well run out of time. It was originally built by the Count of Boulogne and his wife Mahaut, and now you can walk through the vaults and underground passages of this listed building. In the museum you can enjoy 4,000m2 of antique Grecian vases, Egyptian sarcophogi, renaissance coins, Eskimo and Aleutian masks and many exhibits brought back from Oceania 100 years ago by the sailors of Boulogne.

Le Beffroi
(attached to the Town Hall)

The bellfry is the oldest monument in the Old Town. It was once used as a dungeon and symbolises communal liberty. It is worth visiting if only for the breath-taking views of the port, the town and the sea. Access is from the ground floor of the town hall. Entrance is free.

Basilique Notre-Dame,
Enc de l'Evêche

This 'hybrid' cathedral was collectively inspired by St Paul's Cathedral, St Peter's in Rome, the Panthéon and Les Invalides in Paris. It is located on top of a 12th century maze of crypts and its dome dominates Boulogne town. It has 14 chambers containing vestiges of the 3rd century Roman temple and many bejewelled religious artifacts.

Les Remparts

Did you know that Boulogne is a walled city?
Not many do. The 13th century fortifications

surround the cobbled streets of the Haute Ville. Built by the Count of Boulogne on the foundations of a Gallo-Roman wall, it has four gates and seventeen turrets. Take a peaceful stroll along the ramparts to enjoy the panoramic views of the town and its coastline.

Le Bellfroi

The Cathedral Dome dominates the town of Boulogne

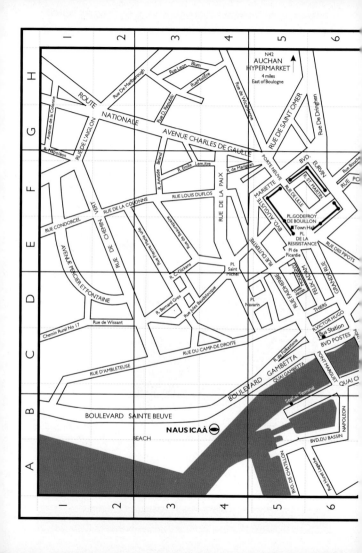

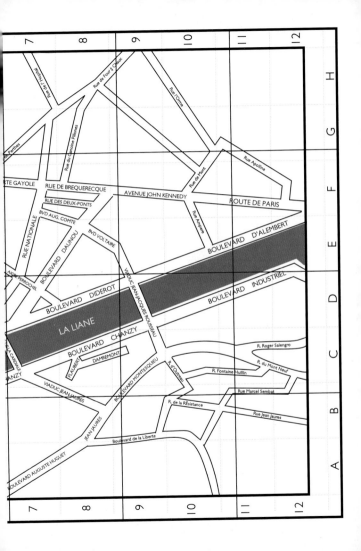

Auchan
RN42
6220 St-Martin Boulogne

Map Ref:	Follow H5 direction
Bus No:	8
English:	No
Tasting:	No
Payment:	£, 💳 💳
Parking:	Yes
Open:	Monday to Saturday 8.30am to 10pm
Closed:	Sunday

BEST HYPERMARKET GROUP

How To Get There

From the port of Boulogne initially follow signs to St Omer and St Martin-B then signs for St Martin B-Centre. Follow the N42 straight through the town on the Route de St Omer and cross over the roundabout with MacDonalds on the right. Cross over the next roundabout too, continue for 1.5 miles, take the exit Centre Commercial direct to Auchan and follow signs to Centre Commercial. Auchan will loom up ahead of you.

Auchan Hypermarket is generally considered the biggest and the best place to visit in Boulogne for general supermarket shopping. It is brightly lit, very spacious, and very colourful.

Together with its sister branch in Calais, Auchan has won the Best Hypermarket Group for its breadth of products and competitive pricing.

As is typical of French hypermarkets, Auchan dominates a shopping complex housing many small retail shops and service outlets.

For detailed product listings and recommendations , please see the entry for Auchan in the Calais section.

For a list of spirits please refer to the Tipple Table.

Centre E. Leclerc
Boulevard Industrial
de la Liane,
62230 Outreau

Map Ref:	D12
Bus No:	22
English:	No
Tasting:	No
Payment:	£, 💳 💳
Parking:	Yes
Open:	Monday to Saturday 9am to 8pm
Closed:	Sunday

How To Get There

From the port turn immediate right and follow the signs to Z I de la Liane on Boulevard Chanzy (alongside the canal on the left).

Continue for about a quarter of a mile and Centre E. Leclerc is on the right hand side.

We like to refer to this supermarket as 'baby Auchan'. It is bright and spacious and similar in many ways to Auchan from its decor to the products and even prices.

However its smaller size means it is a far more intimate place to shop.

A small section of the supermarket has been designed to look like a cellar complete with dimmed lighting - not surprisingly it is called 'La Cave'. It is here that the quality wines are kept. These are exclusively French wines, champagnes and quality liqueurs.

There are some foreign wines too but they are kept on the shelves in the main shop with the cheaper French plonk!

Le Chais
Bréquercque Village,
49 rue des Deux Ponts
Boulogne

Map Ref:	F8
Bus No:	9 & 14 (stop close by)
English:	A little
Tasting:	Some
Payment:	£, VISA ●
Parking:	Yes
Open:	9am-7pm
Closed:	12pm-2.30pm each day & all day Sunday and Monday

How To Get There

From the Boulogne port cross over the bridge and veer right at the lights. Continue straight on (Boulevard Dannau).

At the lights (BP on the right) continue into Boulevard Beaucerf and take the first left turning. Le Chais is on the right hand side.

Underneath the arches of Boulogne's railway station is Le Chais, a large warehouse style cash and carry. As is typical of French owned wine outlets, the range of wines is predominantly French. The selection is larger than that of the Calais branch. Wines are generally sold in boxes of six or by the mixed dozen with incentives of free wines with bulk purchases.

Le Chais describe themselves as, 'A cellar for those who appreciate fine wines'. With the majority of wines at around £4.00 or over and with names such as **Jaboulet**, **Jadot** and **Chapoutier** jostling for attention, this would be an apt description.

For some recommendations and a product listing refer to the Le Chais' entry in the Calais section.

Cave Paul Herpe Wine Merchant

Cave Paul Herpe
85 rue Pasteur, St Martin
Boulogne

Map Ref:	Follow H5 direction
Bus No:	9
English:	Not much
Tasting:	En vrac
Payment:	£, 💳 💳
Parking:	Yes
Open:	9am-12.15pm & 2pm-7pm daily
Closed:	Sunday

How To Get There

From Boulogne port follow signs to St. Omer and St. Martin- B. Follow the N42 straight through the town on the Route de St Omer.

Turn left into Rue de la Colonne and then take 3rd right into Rue Pasteur.

This little outlet specialises in the wines of just one region of France - the Languedoc. Here you can discover the delights of this Southern area of France. On offer are the familiar Languedoc's names - such names as **Fitou, Corbières, Minervois** and **La Clape**, many of which are from vineyards exclusive to Cave Paul Herpe. Certainly the wines that emerge from the Languedoc vines tend to be the best value French wines. For example you can purchase an **AOC La Clape, Château de Capitoul '94** for less than £3.00 or a full bodied **Corbières Château Auris AOC** for just over £3.00. Also on offer is a **Muscat de Riversaltes** at £4.69 - the kind of sweet fortified wine (aperitif) that this region was originally famous for. It has a spicy bouquet and a distinctly floral palate. Another attraction of this outlet is that you can buy wines here 'en vrac'. The wine is contained in huge cylinders and by use of a tap, you can pour wine into plastic containers. Prices start from around £1.50 per litre for a Vins de Table wine and around £2.75 per litre for an AOC Coribières, Minervois or Fitou. You can even purchase **Muscat de Riversaltes en vrac** for £5.15 per litre (in a minimum 33 Litre containers available at the outlet).

Mille Vignes Wine Merchant

Mille Vignes
90 Rue Carnot, 62930 Wimereux

Map Ref:	follow B1
Bus No:	-
English:	Yes
Tasting:	Yes
Payment:	£, VISA ●●
Parking:	Opposite the shop and off street
Open:	Tuesday - Saturday 10am-1.30pm & 2.30-7.00pm Sunday 10am-1pm
Closed:	Monday, not December

How To Get There

From Calais port Take the A16 motorway towards Boulogne - Turn off at Junction 4 - Wimilles/Wimereux Nord. Follow signs for Centre of Wimereux.

From Boulogne port: Take D940 coast road in the direction of Wimereux/Calais.

BEST CROSS-CHANNEL WINE OUTLET 1998

BEST CROSS-CHANNEL WHITE WINE 1998
Bourgogne Chardonnay, Olivier Leffaivve 1995 - FF39 - £4.33

BEST CROSS-CHANNEL RED WINE 1998
Domaine St. Gayan 1995 Rosteau Côtes du Rhône Villages - FF39 - £4.33

The owner of Mille Vignes, is an Englishman with a palate, it seems, for fine French wine. It was through this passion that the idea of a wine outlet in France selling quality French wines to the English was created. Mille Vignes was opened by the Mayor of Wimereux two years ago. The owner, a silversmith working in England, leaves the management of Mille Vignes to Nick Sweet another Englishman and a connoisseur of wines. Nick is very approachable and is happy to guide you through the selection.

The speciality is indeed French wines, those from the Rhône, Loire, white Burgundy, Claret originating from family owned Domaines and Châteaux. Amid their unusual and consistently good selection there are many wines to recommend.

Here are a few:

Domaine du Poujol Rosé 1996 26FF (£2.88) - Firm, dryish, tempered with strawberry fruit.
Château La Boutignane Corbières 1996 23FF (£2.55) - Spicy, floral aromas and spicy overtones.
Domaine du Poujol Vin de Pays de L'Herault 27FF (£3.00) - Best decanted, but has soft strong fruit flavours. Authentic and good.
Rasteau Domaine St Gayan 1995 39FF (£4.33) - Dark in colour, pungent with lots of fruit yet earthy and savoury on the tongue.

Domaine du Raifault Chinon 1995 39FF (£4.33) - A rounded wine ripe with raspberry fruit.
Domaine de Font-Sane Gigondas 1995 69FF (£7.66) - Sweet, spicy perfumed scents with rich meaty flavours, well balanced.
Château Puy Guilhem Fronsac 1995 59FF (£6.55) - Lightish but intense and penetrating.
Le Brun de Neuville Brut Champagne 1995 95FF (£10.55) - Gentle with medium depth.
Julienas 1996, J Gonard et Fils 41FF (4.55) - Intense and zingy.
Château Landereau 1995, Bordeaux Superieur 39FF (£4.33) - An easy going wine, soupy in style.
Bourgogne Chardonnay 1995, Olivier Leflaive 39FF (£4.33) - An excellent value wine, with white flower and summer fruit aromas, a soft, intense, plump, well balanced classic white wine.

Mille Vignes

A Summary of the Bargain Basement Wines

Red wine under £1.00	Price	Outlet
Vin de Pays de L'Herault	0.55	Aldi
Dmn Preiure de la Serre Vin de Pays de L'Aude	0.55	Continent
Côtes du Roussillon	0.63	Aldi
Cuvée des Molières	0.84	Franglais
Courbières Rouge AOC	0.86	Carrefour
Cuvée de Patron	0.86	Franglais
Roquefeuilles Vin de Pays de L'Aude	0.87	Tesco
Tesco French Wine	0.87	Tesco
Vin de Pays de L'Aude	0.88	Auchan
Tesco Romanian Country Red	0.91	Tesco
Vin de Pays de L'Aude Adeline	0.91	Pidou
Carré de Vigne Tetra Brik, Vin de Table 1L	0.93	Auchan
Minervois AOC	0.94	Carrefour
Vino Rosso	0.99	Wine & Beer Co
Merlot Gamza	0.99	Wine & Beer Co
Cabernet Novoselska Gamza	1.00	Eastenders
Merlot Villa Rica 1994	1.00	Eastenders

White wine under £1.00	Price	Outlet
Blanc de Blanc Fruit de Mer	0.55	Aldi
Canterrane Vin de Table Tetra Brik 1L	0.66	Auchan
Stowels of Chelsea Chenin Blanc	0.78	Tesco
Grappe d'Or Blanc Moelleux	0.84	Franglais
Vin Blanc Sec Festignere	0.85	Pidou
Tesco French White	0.87	Tesco
Fruits de Mer Vin de Table	0.94	Tesco
Tesco Hock	0.94	Tesco
Millbrook English Table Wine	0.99	Wine & Beer Co
Aligote Ugni Blanc	0.99	Wine & Beer Co
Vino Bianco	0.99	Wine & Beer Co
Dry White Olympus	1.00	Eastenders
Don Mamede, Vinho Regional Estremadura	1.00	Eastenders
Gros Plant VDQS	0.99	Tesco

Rosé wine under £1.00	Price	Outlet
Vin du Pays du Var	0.86	Carrefour
Jean Duvignoble Vin de Table Rosé	0.96	Tesco
Chapparrall Rosé	0.99	Beer Lovers
Griseley. Rémy Pannier, Erde	1.00	Eastenders
Rosé Valentin, Rémy Pannier, Erde	1.00	Eastenders

Sparkling wine under £1.00	Price	Outlet
Doriant Brut & Demi Sec	0.81	Franglais
Pol Remy Brut & Demi Sec	0.83	Tesco
Baron de Rothberg Brut & Demi Sec	0.91	Franglais
Moscato Spumante	0.97	Tesco
Spumante	0.99	Wine & Beer
Vin Mosseaux, dry, medium or sweet	0.99	Wine & Beer
Lovely Bubbly	1.00	Eastenders

Champagne under £6.00	Price	Outlet
Amarande Brut	5.88	Auchan

That's The Spirit - The Tipple Table

We recommend that you use up your Duty Free allowance to buy spirits and then top up in France. The following table lists 100 of the most popular products in alphabetical order. Where possible we have included the average UK price so that you can see your savings at a glance.

Prices have been converted to Sterling for your convenience.

Please bear in mind that prices do tend to fluctuate, usually within a 5% band. The table that follows is a guide to what you can expect.

TIPPLE TABLE - PRICES ARE IN £ STERLING

PRODUCT	% vol	Average UK price	Tesco	Auchan	Carrefour	Continent	Victoria wine	Pidou
Aberlour Scotch Whisky 10yrs 70cl	43		12.77	12.54		12.54		
Absolut Vodka 70cl	40			9.51	9.44	9.39	9.44	
Bacardi White Rum 70cl	37.5	10.99	8.46		8.15	8.22		
Baileys Irish Cream 70cl	17	11.49	7.37	7.51	7.44	7.44	10.55	
Ballantines 70cl	40		8.43	8.93	8.55	8.85		8.23
Beefeater London Dry Gin 70cl	40	12.44	8.92		8.09	8.61	9.86	10.00
Bells 8yrs 70cl	40	11.99	9.76	9.30		9.30	10.63	
Benedictine 70cl	40	16.99	10.98		11.83			
Black & White Scotch Whisky 70cl	40			8.05		8.84	9.00	9.55
Bombay Sapphire London Dry Gin 70cl	40			12.69	12.27	12.68	11.21	12.54
Calvados 70cl	40					7.44		9.28
Campari 1L	25		10.17	8.51	8.51	8.53	8.88	
Canadian Club Whisky 70c	40					10.41	10.17	
Canadian Mist Whisky 70cl	40			7.77	7.77	10.49	10.17	
Captain Morgan 70cl	40	11.59	9.31					
Cardhu Single Malt 70cl	40	17.22	17.22		17.11	18.15	21.11	
Chivas Regal Scotch Whisky 12 yrs 70cl	40			15.31	15.31	15.33	23.33	16.65
Cinzano Bianco 1L *75cl	16	*4.99				4.58	*3.33	
Cinzano Rosso 1L	16				4.63	4.58	4.44	
Clan Campbell 1L	40					10.87		
Clan Campbell 70cl	40				7.97		7.96	
Cles Des Ducs Armagnac 70cl	40			8.08	10.55	9.56		10.11
Cognac Bisquit Classique 70cl	40				11.80	10.79	11.77	
Cointreau 70c	40	15.99	13.88	10.23	11.48	11.66	12.22	
Courvoisier Cognac 70cl	40	20.34	13.33	12.11		13.11	16.66	11.00
Croft Tawny Port 75cl	19.5			5.50		5.17	5.17	8.54
Cutty Sark Scotch Whisky 70cl	40				8.54	8.54		
Dimple 70cl	40				18.65	18.05		
Drambuie 70cl	40	17.69	15.00		14.91	18.05		
Dubonnet 1L	16	7.48		4.95	4.95			4.95

That's The Spirit - The Tipple Table

PRODUCT	% vol	Average UK price	Tesco	Au:han	Carrefour	Continet	Victoria wine	Pidou
Eristoff Vodka 70cl	37.5			6.38		6.38	6.38	7.15
Famous Grouse Scotch Whisky 70cl	40	11.49	9.98	5.69	9.98	9.69	10.55	10.59
Four Roses Bourbon Scotch Whisky 70cl	40			5.02		8.87	8.42	9.28
Gilbey's London Dry Gin 70cl	37.5				6.38	6.38		7.42
Glen Rogers Scotch Whisky 70cl	40				9.38		8.51	9.99
Glen Turner Pure Malt 8yrs 70cl	40				9.25		9.25	9.32
Glenfiddich 70cl	40	13.44	13.77	14.17	13.70	16.28	18.88	
Glenlivet 12 yrs 70cl	40	19.99	15.00	15.70	14.38	15.70	17.24	
Glenmorangie 10yrs 70cl	40	18.77		19.86	18.33	20.00		
Gold River 8yrs 70cl	30				6.62		6.60	6.61
Gordon's London Dry Gin 1L	37.5	14.79	9.49		11.10	12.77	9.44	7.97
Gordon's London Dry Gin 70cl	37.5			7.13	7.78	7.13	15.00	11.73
Grand Marnier Liqueur 70cl	40	17.99	15.22	11.29		11.29	7.86	8.56
Grants Whisky 70cl	40	10.15	7.65	7.85		7.61	7.10	
Haig Gold Label 70cl	40				7.08			
Harveys Bristol Cream 1L	17.5	7.99	7.00			8.66		
Hennessy Cognac 70cl	40	13.11		13.33				
J&B Whisky 70c	40			9.96		9.88	9.37	10.42
Jack Daniels Whisky 70cl	43	16.99	12.22	11.77	11.77	12.11	13.88	13.03
Jameson Irish Whiskey 70cl	40	11.99	10.16	9.65	9.73	9.65	10.51	
Janneau Grand Armagnac 70cl	40	9.44	10.54		10.66			
Jim Bean Bourbon 70cl	40	10.97		9.83				
Johnnie Walker 1L	40	14.33	13.15	13.22	13.57	13.70	15.55	
Johnnie Walker Black Label Whisky 70cl	40							
Johnnie Walker Red Label Whisky 70cl	40			9.00	11.00	9.03	12.22	9.40
Kahlua Liqueur 70cl	26	10.17	8.65		8.65	9.44		
Knockando Whisky 70cl	43	18.33	17.40	17.21	17.21	17.17		
Label 5 70cl	40			7.55		7.71	7.43	
Lambs Navy Rum 70cl	40	10.79	9.26			9.00		
Laphroaig 70cl	43	21.99	18.77	9.11				
Long John Scotch Whisky 70cl	40			7.48	7.52	18.07 / 7.54	8.47	
Macallan 70cl	43			19.99	20.22	19.44		
MacArthur's 70cl	40							
Malibu White Rum 1L	21	10.99	8.50		6.65			
Martell 3 Star Cognac 70cl	40	19.98	12.77	14.93	8.88			

That's The Spirit – The Tipple Table

PRODUCT	% vol	Average UK price	Tesco	Auchan	Carrefour	Continent	Victoria wine	Pidou
Martini Bianco 1L	16	5.99	4.97	4.94	4.85	5.76		
Martini Rosé 1L	16	5.99	4.94	4.88		5.37		
Martini Rosso 1L	16	5.99	4.94	4.94	4.83	5.22		
Muscat Riversaltes 1L	15.5			2.99		3.65		
Negrita Rum 1L	40			7.34		7.20	7.95	
Noilly Prat 1L*75cl	18	*5.99	*5.02	5.52	5.52	5.52		
Old Lady's London Dry Gin 70cl	37.5			6.59		7.22	6.09	
Old Nick White Rum 70cl	40				5.20		6.60	
Old Virginia Bourbon 70cl	40				7.87		5.44	
Pastis 51 Pastis 51 1L	45				10.69		8.87	8.09
Pernod 1L	40					10.70		
Pernod 70cl	40	10.88	10.32	9.12	8.33		10.66	
Pimms 70cl	25	11.55	8.22				9.44	11.36
Red Runner Whisky 70c	24				3.21	7.36		
Remy Martin VSOP 70cl	40	25.79	18.17	19.60	19.66	9.25	22.22	8.32
Ricard Pastis 70cl	45			8.27		4.61		10.55
Rozés Tawny Porto 75cl	20			5.02	4.62	5.22		
Sandeman Port 75cl	19	9.59		6.76	6.98	6.75	8.22	7.56
Smirnoff Vodka 70cl	37.5		7.26	5.34	5.68	8.37	8.37	
St James White Rum 70CL	40				10.58	11.11	12.31	
Southern Comfort 70cl	40	14.99	12.31	11.66			12.31	
Teachers Scotch Whisky 70cl	40	11.69	8.87		8.33			
Tia Maria 70cl	26.5			11.86	12.01		11.00	
Vladivar Vodka 1L	37.5	12.64	9.10					
Warninks Advocaat 70cl	17.2	9.89	7.66			7.91		
White Horse Scotch Whisky 70cl	40	10.99	8.33	7.83		7.84		
White & Mackay Special Reserve 70cl	40	11.29	8.50		8.1	7.43		
Wild Turkey No.8 Bourbon Whisky 70cl	43.4			8.24	10.43	10.44	12.65	
William Lawson Scotch Whisky 70cl	40				8.07	8.07	9.42	
William Peel 1L	40				9.80	9.35		
William Peel No. 6 70cl	40			7.22	7.10	6.94		
Wyborowa Vodka 70cl	40			8.21	8.88	8.18		
Zubrowka Vodka 70cl	40			9.53	9.53	9.98		

Which Wine?

France is one of the leading wine producing countries and this is reflected in the French outlets where most, if not all, of their selection is French. With so much to choose from, it helps to know a little about French wine.

Firstly, inspect the label for an indication and therefore an assurance of the quality of the wine. The best wines of the regions have **Appéllation Contrôlées** on the label which gives a guarantee of the origin, supervision of production method, variety of grape and quantity produced.

Less controlled but nevertheless wines of good value, are listed as **Vins Délimités de Qualité Supérieure (VDQS)** and are worth trying. There are also the **Vins de Pays**. These are country wines, more widely found in the South of France, which do not specify the exact location of the vineyard but are almost always worth trying and often offer the best value for money. Good

examples are **Vin de Pays du Gard** and the wines from **Côtes de Gascogne**. Further down the ladder are the **Vins de Table**. They are varied in quality but are so cheap that they are worth a gamble. You could be surprised for as little at FF5-12.00 (55p-£1.33).

We have very broadly categorised the wine growing areas into seven major regions.
These are: **Alsace, Burgundy, Bordeaux, Champagne, Loire, Midi** and **Rhône**.

Which Wine?

Alsace

The Alsace is situated in Eastern France on the German border.

The wine labels from this area differ from the rest of France by calling the wine by the name of the grape rather than the area e.g. **Gewürztraminer, Riesling**.

If a label reads **Alsace AC**, this is the standard Alsace wine which is typically Germanic in character, often being aromatic and fruity, but drier than its German equivalent.

A label with **Alsace Grand Cru** printed on it indicates a higher quality and only the four most highly regarded grape types can be used in its making and they are: **Gewürztraminer, Riesling** (not to be confused with the German wine of the same name), **Tokay Pinot** and **Muscat**. These are medium priced white wines with reliable quality and are generally dry to medium dry.

The Alsation wines are great aperitifs and also combine well with fish, poultry, salads or with a summer meal.

Expect to pay: 15-30 francs (£1.66-£3.33) per bottle.

Bordeaux

Bordeaux is in the South West region of France with the Dordogne region on its eastern border and the Atlantic ocean on the west.

The term Claret refers to the red dry wines of this region and wines such as Médoc, St. Emillion and Pomerol which are in the lower price range.

There are also numerous wines known by the name of Château. Quality, especially at the lower end, can be variable. Claret goes well with meat, chicken and cheese.

Expect to pay: From as little as 14 francs (£1.55) per bottle, to more than 100 francs (£12.50) for a top class Château.

Which Wine?

Situated between Bordeaux and the Dordogne valley is an area called **Bergerac.**

Bergerac has a complete range of wines of its own; most commonly **Bergerac** (red, rosé and dry white), **Côtes de Bergerac** (red and medium sweet wine), **Monbazillac** (sweet white) and **Pécharmant** (very fine red).

Expect to pay: 10-16 francs (£1.11-£1.77) for the Bergerac. 30 francs (£3.33) for Monbazillac.

Burgundy

Burgundy is an area of France south-east of Paris running from Chablis at the northern end, down through to Lyon at the southern end. About 75% of the wine production in this region is red with the remainder white.

It is worth noting the area on the label when choosing a Burgundy wine since the more exact the area, the finer the wine is likely to be. The best are labelled 'Grand Cru', followed by 'Premier Cru', 'Villages', a specified region and finally, the most basic will have just Burgundy. The best known of the whites is Chablis which is in the higher price bracket. The Côte de Beaune produces some of the finest such as Meursault and some good light dry wines come from Mâconnais such as Mâcon Blanc and Pouilly Fuissé. All Burgundy white wines are dry and are an ideal accompaniment for fish.

The finest red Burgundy wine comes from the Côtes de Nuits such as Nuits St Georges and the Côtes de Beaune namely Pommard, Volnay and Monthélie. These are best drunk with meat, game and cheese.

Expect to pay: 35-70 francs (£3.88-£7.77) These wines tend to be reliable in this price bracket.

Best known of the reds in the South of this region is

Which Wine?

Beaujolais. Beaujolais is divided into the standard Beaujolais AC, Beaujolais Superieur which denotes a slightly higher alcohol content and Beaujolais-Villages which is an appéllation controllée (quality control) given to about 40 villages and considered to be of superior quality

The most prestigious of the Beaujolais wines bear the name of one of the ten communes (Crus). These are worth noting since you will come across them practically everywhere. These are **Saint-Amour, Juliénas, Chénas, Moulin-à-Vent, Fleurie, Chiroubles, Morgon, Brouilly, Côte de Brouilly and Régnié** (the most recently created, but least distinguished Cru).

These are medium priced red dry fruity wines with the Villages and Communes especially reliable and should be drunk young and served slightly chilled.

Expect to pay: 10-25 francs (£1.11-£2.77) for basic Beaujolais AC. 15-45 francs (£1.87-£5.62) per bottle for Beaujolais- Villages or named Commune.

Midi
(Languedoc Roussillon & Provence)
This region stretches from north east of Marseilles down to the west of Perpignan bordering Spain.

Wines from this region, such as Minervois and Corbières represent good value dry reds. The Vin de Pays (sometimes referred to as Country Wines) of the area offer the best value of all. The label will always show the Vin de Pays description followed by the region.

Expect to pay: 6-20 francs (66p-£2.22) per bottle and a little more if VDQS (Vins Délimités de Qualité Supérieure) is printed on the label.

Which Wine?

Rhône

This area is located south of the Burgundy region and continues due south to the Mediterranean near Marseillesand. The region generally produces robust, full bodied wines.

There is the standard Côtes du Rhône and the Côtes du Rhône Villages which is famous for its dry red wine. If the wine is attributable to a named village (which is shown on the label) the chances are it will be better quality but naturally more expensive. Côtes du Rhône wines accompany cheese and poultry dishes very well.

Expect to pay: 8-20 francs (88p-£2.22) for Côtes du Rhône label wines. 20-30francs (£2.22-£3.33) for Côtes du Rhône Villages.

Loire

The Loire wine region starts at Nantes on the Western Atlantic coast of France and follows the Loire river east to Orléans where it cuts back southeast to Sancerre. The majority of wines produced in this area are white.

The Loire offers the widest variety of wine of any area in France and all have a certain refreshing quality that comes from the northerly position of most of the major Loire vineyards and the character of the soil.

Amongst the many well-known names from this area are Muscadet, Gros Plant Du Nantais, Poully-Fumé and Sancerre being examples of dry whites, and Anjou which is well known for its Rosé.

The Rosé wine is very versatile and can be drunk throughout the course of the meal. The whites are best with fish and salads.

Although named wines are generally a better buy, in our experience it is especially true for **Muscadet** where we recommend either a named or 'sur lie' over the ordinary Muscadet.

Which Wine?

Expect to pay: 8-15 francs (88p-£1.66) for Gros Plant.
10-22 francs (£1.11-£2.44) for Muscadet.
35-39 francs (£3.88-£4.33) for Sancerre & Pouilly Fumé
10-16 francs (£1.11-£1.77) for Anjou Rosé wines.

If you prefer a medium dry wine then try the Vouvray at 20-25 francs (£2.50-£3.12). Vouvray is also available as a sparkling wine.

Champagne

Champagne is situated north east of Paris with Reims and Epernay at the heart of this region renowned for the most famous sparkling wines in the world. These are usually sold under a brand name e.g. Bollinger, Moët et Chandon, Mumm, Veuve Clicquot etc. which are nearly always dry.

If you do not like dry wines, then ask for a demi-sec or even a rosé Champagne. These wines are generally drunk at parties, celebrations or through a meal.

Only wine made in the champagne area is entitled to be called Champagne. Other wine of this type is referred to as 'sparkling' wine but some have Méthode Champenoise on the label which means made in the Champagne method'.

Expect to pay: 50-70 francs (£5.55-£7.77) for lesser known brands.
115 francs (£12.77) upwards for well-known brands.

Here For The Beer?

Without a doubt, the best bargain to be had in France is the beer. With savings of up to 50 per cent beer drinkers are certainly not bitter !

Fortunately, beer is in abundance in Calais and Boulogne and the most widely available beers tend to be continental. The average continental beer has an alcoholic content of at least 4.5% which is more than 1% stronger than the average British bitter.

You may find 'promos' offering beers cheaply but these could be lower alcohol beers such as Kúnigsbier or Brandeberg which both retail at around £2.80 for 24 bottles but both have an alcoholic volume of only 2.80%!

The majority of continental beers are light in colour and are best served chilled. These are sold in 25cl bottles which equates to just under half a pint (0.43).

The highest alcoholic beers tend to be from Belgium. The more popular ones include Hoegaarden (5% ABV) known as either Witbier or Bière Blanche meaning White Beer and refers to its naturally cloudy appearance. Although in Britain cloudiness is usually associated with the beer being past its best, in this case, it is due to its production process and ingredients: barley, unmalted wheat, Styrian and Kent hops, coriander and curacao. As it brews, the top-fermenting yeast turns the malt to alcohol, but because the wheat is not malted, the starches contribute to the final cloudy appearance.

Possibly the best-known Belgium beers are Trappist beers made by monks in just five Trappist monastery breweries in Belgium. These include Chimay Red (7%) - copper colour and slightly sweet, Chimay White (6.3%) - lots of hop and slightly acidic, Chimay Blue (7.1%) - fruity aromas, Orval (6.2%) - orange hue, with acidity;

Here For The Beer?

Rochefort 6,8,10 (ABVs are 7.3%, 7.5% and 11.3%) - characteristics range from russet colour with a herbal palate, tawny and fruity to dark brown with chocolate and fruity palate respectively.

Pilsner style beers include the mass marketed beers of Jupiler, a dry and soft easy drinking beer and Stella Artois (the biggest brewing company in Belgium) who also make Leffe - an abbey style ale.

France itself has two brewing regions. The first is in the North around the city of Lille, the most well known part being French Flanders. The style of beer produced - **bière de garde** - resembles its Belgian counterparts. Strasbourg, in the East is the other brewing region. The final product is similar to German lagers.

The major French breweries are Kronenbourg/Kanterbrau, Mutzig and Pelforth The latter situated near Lille and owned by Heineken, produces light and dark lagers: Pelforth Blonde (5.8%) and Pelforth Brune (5.2% & 6.5%).

There are also popular beers from 'down under' such as Castlemain XXXX and the sweetish Fosters lager (both 4%) which are widely availabe.

Products from many British breweries also share shelf space in Northern France, especially at British supermarkets such as Tesco and Sainsbury's . These include Shepherd Neame's malty Bishop's Finger (12.5%), John Smith's bitter (4.8% & 4%), Whitbread's creamy headed Boddington's bitter (3.8%), Tetley's creamy, nutty Yorkshire ale (3.6%) and Ireland's earthy, dry Guinness Draught (5%).

Whichever beer you choose your enjoyment will be heightened by the knowledge that it often costs only a half of what you would have paid in the UK!

Here For The Beer?

Yes It's True -
Beer from 11p Per Bottle

Beer	% Vol	£ Price	Outlet
Winny	3.7	11p	Tesco
Facon	4.9	12 p	Auchan
Koenigsbier	2.6	12p	Continent
Brandeberg	2.8	12p	Pidou
Gruber Bieres	4.5	12p	Tesco
Koenigsbier	4.5	13p	Continent
Bière Cruiser	4.9	13p	Pidou
*Hofmeister	3.4	13p	Tesco
Kusterbier	4.7	14p	Aldi
Alsabrau	3.7	14p	Carrefour
Reine de Flanders	n/a	14p	Continent
33 Export	4.8	14p	Continent
Uberland	4.5	14p	Eastenders
Bière Sembrau	3.7	14p	Pidou
Magister	5.0	14p	Tesco
Kanterbrau	4.7	15p	Continent
Bière Sphinx	5.0	15p	Pidou
Bière Kwik Pils	5.0	15p	Pidou
Blondenbrau	4.6	15p	Pidou
Bière Nordik Pils	5.0	15p	Pidou
Bière Magister	5.0	15p	Pidou
Bière Blondy	5.0	15p	Pidou
Bière ASB	5.2	15p	Pidou
Bière Martens Pils	5.0	15p	Pidou
Bière St Omer	5.0	15p	Pidou/Carrefour
Alsatia	5.2	16p	Beer Lovers
Marten's	5.0	16p	Beer Lovers
Bière Blonde Carrefour	4.6	16p	Carrefour
Artenbrau	5.0	16p	Carrefour
St Omer	5.0	16p	Continent
ESP	5.2	16p	Eastenders
Burg Pils	5.3	16p	Pidou
St Omer	5.0	16p	Tesco
Pilsor	4.0	16p	Wine & Beer
Cruiser	5.0	17p	Beer Lovers
Cristalor	4.7	17p	Wine & Beer
Stella Artois-special collectives	5.2	18p	Eastenders
Fischer La Strasbourgeoisie	4.9	18p	Tesco
Semeuse	5.0	18p	Tesco/Continent/Carrefour
Wernesgrüner - 33cl bottles	4.9	20p	Eastenders

*Available only in 50cl quantities. The calculation has been adjusted accordingly.

Here For The Beer?

Beer Labels

What you see on a beer label is what you get. But what do the terms mean? Here are a few terms explained:

Abbey, Abbaye: This suggests a beer made by monks - not so, but the trappist style has been used. Sometimes an abbey will have licensed it.

Ale: An English word meaning a brew made with a top-fermenting yeast - expect a certain fruitiness to its flavour

Bière de Gard: A French phrase for a top-fermented brew with an alcohol content between 4.4-7.5%.

Bitter: An English word implying a depth of hop bitterness. The alcohol content is usually around 3.75-4%. If the world Best or Special is also present the alcohol content is slightly higher at 4-4.75%. If the words Extra Special are present this denotes an alcohol content of 5.5%.

Export: In Germany this means a pale bottom-fermented beer with an alcohol content of 5.25-5.5% Outside Germany this indicates a premium beer.

Ice Beer: The beer has been frozen at some stage.

Lager: A bottom-fermented beer.

Lambic: Wheat beer unique to Belgium. Alcohol content of 4.4%.

Pilsener/Pilsner/Pils: A term generally applied to any golden coloured, dry, bottom-fermenting beer. A classic Pilsner is characterised by the hoppiness of its flowery aroma and dry finish. Its origins are in the CzechRepublic from the town of Pilsen.
Stout: An extra-dark, top-fermenting brew made from roasted malts.

Trappist: An order of monks with 5 breweries in Belgium and 1in the Netherlands. It is illegal to use this term for any other product. Their beers are strong with an alcoholic content of between 6-12%.

Tripel: A Dutch word meaning the strongest beer of the house. These beers are often pale in colour and top fermented.

Weisse/Weissbier, Weizenbier: German for 'white' beer.

Eau, What A Choice!

It's the best thirst quenching drink there is. It's not alcohol but it's a bargain !

Mineral water, (**eau minérale**) both still (**plate**) and sparkling (**gazeuse**) is exceptionally good value for money and substantially cheaper to buy in France. Why this is so is perplexing as unlike alcohol, there is no tax to blame.

There is often a vast selection of different brands at the hypermarkets. Some, such as Evian, Volvic and the comparatively expensive Perrier will be familiar, yet some of the lesser known brands are just as good. For example in Aldi the sparkling River brand is just 22p for 1.5 litres which we believe to be under half the price of the equivalent in the UK. Also in Aldi is a still water - Lucheux - which at 12.5p a 2 litre bottle must merit some space in your boot.In our blind tasting, we sampled a some mineral waters at fridge temperature. Here are a selection of the commonly available mineral waters:

Badoit: Slightly sparkling from the Loire.
Ave Price: FF3.50 (40p) 1L
Comment: Slightly salty

Contrexéville: From Vosges. Reputedly good for the kidneys Has a slightly diuretic effect.
Ave Price: FF2.9 (33p) 1.5L
Comment: Slightly salty.

Evian: From the town of Evian at Lake Geneva.It has a slightly diuretic effect.
Ave Price: FF4.20 (47p) 2L
Comment: Tasteless but quenching.

Perrier: A very well-marketed mineral water from Nîmes. Full of sparkle and is generally used as soda water in France.
Ave Price: FF4.5 (51p) 1L
Comment: Most refreshing with almost no flavour.

River: Sparkling mineral water
Ave Price: FF1.75 (19p) 1.5L
Comment: Slightly chalky on the palate.

Vichy: A sparkler from Vichy.
Ave Price: FF3 (34p) 1.5L
Comment: Like bicarbonate of soda.

Vittel: A still yet rugged mineral water - comes from Nancy.
Ave Price: FF2.80 (32p) 1.5L
Comment: Refreshing and slightly sweet.

Volvic: A still water from Auvergne filtered through volcanic rock.
Ave Price: FF3 (34p) 1.5L
Comment: A smooth silky taste.

Tobacco Prices Up In Smoke!

You can buy 400 cigarettes Duty Free (200 each way)
AND top up in France - dearer than Duty Free but
cheaper than the UK, and there's no limit for personal use !

Product	Duty Free	France	U.K.
Cigarettes	Av. £	Av. £	Av. £
Benson & Hedges	£1.39	£1.99	£3.17
Camel	£1.49	£2.21	£3.17
Dunhill	£1.49	£2.62	£3.17
Gauloises	£1.20	£2.37	£3.20
Gitanes	£1.85	£1.68	£3.17
John Player Special	£1.49	£1.74	£3.00
Lambert & Butler	£1.39	£2.14	£2.79
Marlboro	£1.53	£2.25	£3.17
Philip Morris	£1.49	£2.22	£3.17
Rothmans	£1.49	£2.07	£3.17
Silk Cut	£1.49	£2.25	£3.17
Superkings	£1.40	£2.13	£3.17
Tobacco			
Drum 50g	£2.20	£2.56	£7.00
Golden Virginia 40g *50g	£3.10*	£2.00	£7.47
Old Holborn 40g *50g	£2.10*	£2.25	£7.47
Samson 50g	£2.10	£2.25	£7.37
Cigars x 5			
King Edward Imperial	£2.99	£4.00	£8.90
Villager Export	£2.10	£3.75	£4.60

The above table illustrates the amount of savings that can be made when buying tobacco in Duty Free shops. If you wish to exceed Duty Free allowances, you can top up in France.

Tobacco can be purchased from outlets called 'Tabacs'. These shops are similar to our own newsagents. Cigarette and tobacco prices are state regulated in France when sold through a tabac. This is not true of tobacco sold in cafés, bars and petrol stations where prices tend to be higher. Unlike the UK, French supermarkets do not sell tobacco at all.

Most tabacs are closed on Sundays and bank holidays. Most accept sterling and credit cards.

The Epicurean's Tour of The Shops

When shopping in any French town what stands out is the variety of traditional gastronomic shops, some of which have no comparable counterpart in the UK. It must be a cultural thing but very simply, the French like to specialise

Take the **Boucherie** for example - the butcher. The Boucherie sells all types of meat and poultry - except pork. To buy pork you need to visit the **Charcuterie** - a word meaning cooked meat.

The **Charcuterie** was originally a pork butcher but has evolved into a pork based delicatessen. Indeed, visiting a Charcuterie for the first time will shift your perception of the humble pig 'le cochon' in gastronomic terms forever! Now you will see it as pâté, terrin, rillets, rillons, hams, dried sausages, fresh sausages, pieds de porc, andouillettes boudins noirs et blancs. This pork lovers haven also offers ready made pork meals with a selection of **plats de jour** that just need heating up when you get home.

Horse meat is also popular in France and this is sold in outlets known as **Boucherie Chevaline** - horse meat butcher, generally identifiable by a horse's head sign.

Cheese, a much revered commodity in France, is produced with exacting procedures by the highly skilled maître fromager (master cheese specialist). The shop to visit to really get the feel of the cheese culture at its best is the **Fromagerie** - a specialist cheese shop which will probably have around 300 varieties on sale.

A cross between a delicatessen and a grocery store is the **Epicerie**. The store sells cheese and fresh meat amongst other food products. These days the Epricerie is based a little on the **Supermarché** and an **Alimentation Général** - a general store and has lost its authenticity somewhat.

The Epicurean's Tour of The Shops

Calais and Boulogne both being fishing towns are awash with fresh seafood. You can buy the catch of the day from the **Poissonerie**. This could be a fishmonger or simply a stall.

Another example of specialisation in action is the **Boulangerie** - the bakery. The shelves are stacked with all types of unusual bread and buns and occasionally cakes and quiches too.

But for a fiendishly good selection of cakes and biscuits, it is over to the **Pâtisserie** for specialist cake, flans and tarts. The **Pâtisserie** sometimes sells icecream too.

Sweets, not the commercial pre-wrapped type, but those that are handmade such as bon-bons, nougat and crystallised fruit, have their own home in a **Confiserie** or **Chocolaterie** - a high class sweet or chocolate shop. The products are a little pricey but certainly good quality, delicious and beautifully packaged for you.

For fresh fruit, flowers and vegetables and a myriad of fresh French delights the best place is the **Marché** - outdoor market. These are generally open on a Saturday or Wednesday.

You could of course, by-pass the specialist shops which offer pleasant insightful echoes of French daily life and culture - a shopping experience unlike any you can have in the UK. You could, instead shop in one of the immense **Hypermarché** - hypermarkets. The total anonymity that comes with being one of hundreds of trolley pushers walking around thousands of kilometres of floor space in a state of suspended reality is an experience all of its own!

Say Cheese

Take a glass of your favourite wine, break off a little baguette, fill it with your favourite cheese - Voila! a gastranomic delight.

The inherent passion for wine within the French culture is closely followed by their love for cheese, so much so that France has become renowned for its remarkably large array of cheeses. Incredibly, the number of different varieties is believed to be in excess of 700. Not only do supermarkets dedicate large areas of floor space to their cheese counters, but the French also have specialist cheese shops.

These quaint shops are called **'Fromageries'** (cheese shops) offering cheese in all its colours and consistencies. Though the nasal passages have to grapple with the pungent aroma that hangs heavily in the air, the palate can look forward to a delightful epicurean experience.

It is at the fromagerie that the finest cheeses can be found, thanks to the resident maÓtre fromager (master cheese specialist). His highly skilled job combines all the complexities of cheese selection, storage and especially, the delicate process of 'affinage'. This is the art of ageing a young cheese to maturity so that it is offered on the cheese counter exactly when it is in its prime.

To the uninitiated though, the cheese counter must look like a daunting display of yellow and white hues with the odd shout of blue. No matter how tempting these colours look, one wonders about the taste. Fortunately, it is customary for the supermarkets and fromageries to offer dégustation (sampling) upon request; a service which they happily and routinely provide.

Fromageries to try are **La Maison du Fromage**, 1 rue Andre- Gerschel in Calais or in Boulogne try **Philippe**

Olivier, 43 rue Thiers. Also in Boulogne you can try La Cave du Fromager, 23 rue de Lille which is connected to a speciality cheese restaurant called Restaurant des Fromages situated nearby.

Although it is not possible to list all the cheeses available, some you come across will already be familiar to you, such as Camembert and Brie (especially with the President label) are widely found and happily also at a third less than prices in the UK.

The fromages fermiers (farmhouse cheese) are considered to be the finest of all cheeses. These are made by small producers using milk from their own farm animals. When unpasteurised milk is use this is denoted with the words 'lait cru'. Other varieties to try are:

Le Brin. A small hexagon shaped cheese. Made from cows' milk, it is mild and creamy. The edible rind has a delicate, pleasant aroma. The special method of production leaves the cheese high in calcium and phosphorus.

Cantorel Roquefort. A blue cheese, ripened in the caves of Cambalou for at least 90 days in accordance with its Appellation d'Origine Contrôlée. It is made entirely from sheep's milk and its distinctive taste is best enjoyed with Barsac or Sauternes wines.

Chimay. You may already be familiar with the Belgian Trappist beer of this name. Chimay is also a range of six Belgian Trappist cheeses. Chimay Bière is flavoured with Chimay beer and is a treat for the palate.

Rambol. Decorated with walnuts it looks like a small gateau. Rambol is a smooth cheese with a mellow flavour. Société Roquefort. Creamy in texture and distinguished by its marbled green and ivory colouring.

St. Agur. A creamy blue

veined cheese from the Auvergne.

It has a mild flavour and sits well on a cheese board.

Tartare. A cream cheese spread from Périgord made with garlic and herbs. It comes as a full fat cheese and for slimmers there's Tartare Light with just a third of the calorie content.

Trappe de Belval. Made by nuns at the abbey of Belval located near to Hesdin. It has a rather hard exterior covering concealing a creamy and mild interior.

Serving suggestions:

- Cheese is at its best served at room temperature, remove from the fridge at least one hour before required.
- Allow 2oz per person for a cheese board and 4oz per person for a cheese and wine evening.
- Select 3-4 different types of cheese for an attractive display, especially on a cheese board.

Storage Tips:

Fortunately, most hard cheeses are freezable as long as they are not overmature when frozen. This is not recommended for soft cheeses.

Generally, the following guidelines for fridge storage apply:

- Fresh Cheese (soft cheese) Eat within a few days.
- Blue Cheese Can be kept up to 3 weeks.
- Goats', Ewe's Milk Cheese Will keep for up to two weeks.
- Always store cheese in the lowest part of the fridge wrapped in foil or in an air proof container to prevent drying out.

Fromagerie

French Bread

It's the law! Every French village must have its own boulangerie (bakery) supplying the villagers with freshly baked bread every day of the week.

Governed by French law, the boulangerie emerges as the single most important shop in any village, faithfully providing the villagers with an essential part of their staple diet - bread.

As with all things French an etiquette has evolved around bread. It is generally considered unacceptable to serve bread purchased in the morning in the evening. No self respecting Frenchman would dare to insult his guests in this way. However, left over bread may be used perhaps for dunking into hot chocolate - in specially formulated wide cups - or alternatively can be cooked in soup.

The most famous and popular French bread (both within and outside France) is the ong, thin **baguette** or French stick. It has a uniform length; and its weight - governed by French law - must be 250 grams!

Although the **baguette** is made simply from soft flour, yeast, water and a pinch or two of salt, it has an appealing fluffy texture and can be enjoyed just as well on its own as it can with food. However, its short life span means that it must be consumed soon after it has been baked. To accommodate this, bakeries routinely bake their bread twice a day so that it is always supplied fresh to a very discriminating public.

Other extreme variations on the baguette are the **ficelle** (a word which literally means string). It is the thinnest loaf available. In contrast **un pain** or **Pariesen** is double the size of a baguette. Some compromise is reached with **petit pains** and the **bâtons** which are much shorter than the baguette and similar to large rolls.

French Bread

For breakfast (**le petit dèjeuner**) the French will also enjoy a Continental breakfast (better known in France as **viennoisie**). This includes such delicious treats as the famous pastry style croissant. This familiar crescent shaped roll was Marie Antoinett's inadvertent contribution to the Western breakfast culture. She introduced them to the Parisian Royals in the late 18th century where they proved to be an epicurean hit.

In Marie Antoinette's home country of Vienna, however, the croissant had been making a regular appearance at the breakfast table as early as 1683. It was in this year that the Polish army saved the city from Turkish hands and in celebratio the Viennese baked a crescent shaped creation based on the Ottoman flag - voila, the croissant was born!

The croissant is reminiscent of puff pastry - made with yeast dough and butter and is usually accompanied by some confit (crystallized fruit) or confiture (various flavours of jam). Sometimes it is served with jam, cheese or chocolate and can be savoured hot or cold.

Traditionally, the croissant is dunked by the French into their coffee in specially made wide cups designed for this purpose. This French idiosyncrasy can also be traced back to the late 17th century. The defeated Turks had left some sacks of coffee beans before they left Vienna. These were discovered by a group of Armenian Jews who started the croissant dunking tradition.

There are also many other tempting varieties of unusual styles of bread available at the specialist boulangerie (bakery) or the boulangerie counter of the hypermarket.

French Bread

Here are some suggestions you may like to try:

Pain au chocolat - a croissant style bun imbued with chocolate (delicious when warm).

Brioche. a breakfast bun made from yeast, dough, eggs and butter, giving it a wonderful sweet, buttery aroma and taste.

Couronnes. A baguette style bread in the shape of a ring.

Pain aux noix. An outstanding bread baked with walnuts on the inside and on the crust.

Pain aux olives. A delicious bread with olives and olive oil.

Pain de sègle. Made with rye and wheat.

Pain noir. Wholemeal bread.

Pain de mie. Sliced bread with a soft crust. Used for sandwiches.

Pain de son. Wholemeal bread fortified with bran.

Pain biologique. This bread is baked with organic wholemeal flour.

Pain campagne. Flatter than baguettes but also heavier. They have the advantage of staying fresh for longer.

Pain au Levain/Pain à l'ancienne. Both these names refer to French bread made from sour dough. This is probably one of the oldest styles of French bread there is.

In Calais you can visit **Fred** at Bd Jacquard situated near the Town Hall (map ref: D4)
In Boulogne try **Joly Desenclos**, at 44-46 rue de Lille (vieille ville map ref: F5). Both these boulangeries have tea rooms.

Specialities at the Pâtisserie

If, like the French, you have a sweet tooth then a visit to a Pâtisserie gives a whole new meaning to the phrase 'Let Them Eat Cake'.

In true French style, even the last course of a meal is not the least. Dinner in any French home will always conclude with a sweet, which if not home made will be bought from the **Pâtisserie** - a specialist cake shop.

The **Pâtisserie** may also have a selection of handmade sweets and chocolates .

Like French wines and cheese, different areas of France have their own regional indulgences on offer. For instance, from Provence comes Marrons Glacés and Fruits Glacés: the former is an autumnal treat of chestnuts in vanilla-flavoured syrup; the latter is simply fresh fruit in sugar syrup.

Normandy famous for its apple orchards, unsurprisingly offers **Tarte Normande** a variation of which is **Gratin de Pommes Vallée D'Auge** -

It is no ordinary apple crumble; it is soaked in Calvados (an apple brandy produced in Normandy) and then baked in crème fraîche.

Even the Pas de Calais area has an indigenous tart whose thick pastry has led to the name Tarte au Gros Bord. It is adorned simply with custard and sugar.

Other offerings include: **Gaufres a La Flamande** - waffles powdered with sugar and sometimes served with whipped cream.

Tarte au Fromage - Cheese cake made from eggs and cottage cheese.

Nougat Glacé - From Provence a frozen honey and almond desert.

Pastis Gasconn - Thin pastry, layered between the folds with vanilla sugar and butter and adorned with apple and marinated in Armagnac

Baba au Rhum - A yeast product soaked in rum flavoured syrup. Best eaten with a spoon.

aOther Shopping Ideas

With the pound so strong, shopping in France is altogether cheaper these days. Here are some tips and shopping ideas.

TIP:
Serious bargain hunters should time their trip to France with the French sales. These happen twice a year - in January and in August and generally last between one to two months . you can pick up some fantastic bargains!

TIP:
Also in August is the Braderie. This is like a giant car boot sale all over the town

TIP:
Take a cooler bag with you just in case you want to buy fresh products such as cheese or fish. Your purchases will stay fresher for longer and you will avoid any pungent smells on the journey home.

Jam (Confiture)
There is a vast selection of confiture. In particular, the brand 'Bonne Maman' which is available in the UK can be found for a third to half the price in the main supermarkets, including Tesco.

Cous Cous
Lovers of cous cous will be pleased to know that you can buy it at half the UK price. Carrefour was the cheapest outlet for this commodity at FF4.95 (62p) for a 1kg pack with other supermarkets close behind. In the UK cous cous is usually sold in half kilo packs for the same price!

Anchovies
You get a wider selection of anchovies, and at half price in France- good value at the hypermarkets.

Peanuts (Cacahuètes)
Look out for peanuts - 30% cheaper than the UK price!

Other Shopping Ideas

Cider (Cidre)

On French supermarket shelves, and in some cash & carries, you will find both French and UK ciders on sale. There are subtle differences between the two, notably that French cider tends to contain less alcohol, around 2.4% as opposed to 5%+ for the British ciders. British ciders such as Strongbow and Bulmers are generally available in France at about half the UK price .

Pasta

There are certain brands of pasta such as Isabella and Monte Regal available in the supermarkets that represent very good value for money. For instance all shapes of Isabella pasta costs around 52p per kilo compared to a similar pasta in the UK which costs 95p.

Rice (Riz) Long grain rice can often be found for under FF5 (50p) per kilo in French supermarkets. Comparable rice in the UK is around 99p.

Mustard (Moutard)

Not only is mustard substantially cheaper in France than in the UK, but there is also a much wider selection. For the sake of price comparison, we will use Dijon mustard which is widely available in both countries. Prices start at FF1.75 (22p) for 370g jar of Dijon mustard compared to a typical UK price of 59p for 250g.

English mustard is slightly hotter than Dijon mustard. Try 'seeded' Dijon mustard; it has a particularly delicate flavour.

Filtered Coffee - (Café Moulu)

Fans of filtered coffee will be pleased to know that this product is available widely and at half the UK prices. Try the taste of even the cheapest brands of filtered coffee and you will not be disappointed. A 1kg (4 x 250g pack) can be found for as little as FF29.00 (£3.62). Try the Arabica brand.

Other Shopping Ideas

Chocolate Milkshake Drinks
The Nestlé Nesquick drinks are normally substantially cheaper in all French supermarkets - typically around £2.47 for 1 kilo. In the UK the standard 225gm Nesquick drink retails for around £1 (equivalent to £4 per kilo).

This represents a 40% saving on the UK supermarket price.

Other French chocolate drinks worth trying are Schovit 800g (in Aldi) and Goucao/Opticao 800g (at most supermarkets) which cost around FF9.45 and FF10.85 respectively. Not only do the prices compare favourably but they are also very tasty and a hit with the kids.

Fruit Juice (Jus de Fruit)
Generally, fruit juice is a third less in France. This is especially true of brands such as Recre, Goldhorn and Lagona ranging from 29p-43p per 1 litre carton. In the UK

the price range would be 59p-89p. In Aldi, rue Mollien we came across 20cl carton orange drinks which are ideal for lunch boxes at the amazing price of 9p per carton! The name of this product is Orangen and can be purchased in packs of 10 for FF7.45 (90p) - under half the price of the nearest UK equivalent.

Crisps (Les Chips)
Crisps are known as 'Les Chips' in France and are generally of a reasonable quality. The big packs are very economical.

In particular Aldi stocks ready salted, paprika and bolognaise flavoured crisps in 200g packets (equivalent to 10 small packets in the UK) for under FF3 (32p).

From all the crisps sampled, these were the least greasy, and the tastiest - ideal for your parties.

Other Shopping Ideas

Olives

In general olives (both black and green) are about 30% cheaper in the French supermarkets. In Aldi try the Olives Vertes Beldi which we found very tasty. Other hypermarkets also have a tasty range of olives. They are great in a baguette with camembert and make a filling snack.

Olive Oil (Huile d'olives)

The finest French olive oils - like French wines - come from named origins and even Appellations controllées. They have a gentle flavour tempered with slight sweetness and are fabulous as condiments, but not are suitable for cooking with. These olive oils have low acidity (sometimes as little as 0.2%) which is significant because acidity affects the rate at which the oil deteriorates. Labels of assured finest quality to look out for are 'Huile de Provence' and 'Huile d'Olives Nyons' (the latter is subject to quality control with its own Appellation d'Origine. This sort of quality is expensive and could be up to £30.00 in the UK (less in France). Generally, you are likely to purchase brands that are commercialy blended. Look for either Extra Virgin (Vierge) or First Cold Pressing (Premier Presson Froid) whose acidity is never more than 1%, but is better still at 0.5%, Fine Virgin olive oil at 1.5% or less, and Ordinary Virgin olive oil whose acidity level is 3%. This sort of quality olive oil in the UK is rarely below £6.00 per litre yet in France the price is generally around FF28.00 (£3.50).

Fish (Poisson)

Being fishing ports, both Calais and Boulogne are rich with fish restaurants. If you have enjoyed a fish or seafood meal, you may be inclined to buy your own to take home. The hypermarkets have fish and seafood sections or better still, you can visit a fish monger (poissonnerie).

Other Shopping Ideas

The prices generally for fish and seafood products tend to be around 10% cheaper in France.

Pots & Pans

You may already be familiar with the names 'Le Creuset' and 'Tefal'. These two popular quality brands of pots and pans are both manufactured in France. You can purchase these in the French hypermarkets and supermarkets for as little as half the UK price. For example, the Le Creuset 20cm saucepan is typically sold in the UK for around £33.00 yet it is available at French hypermarkets at around FF127 (£15.50).

Poissonnerie

Other Shopping Ideas

Mountain Bikes (VTT)

Although we are unable to give a true comparison on mountain bikes, we can say that the hypermarkets do have good value bikes. Adult mountain bikes start at under £100 and children's mountain bikes can be found for around £40.

It is difficult to find these prices in the UK.

Floor Tiles

Situated next door to most hypermarket complexes is a DIY shop called 'Leroy Merlin' specialising in DIY products. DIY enthusiasts will be pleased to know that the average price of floor and wall tiles can be up to half the UK price. Particularly good value were Terracotta floor tiles at just over £5.00 per square metre. Terracotta Pots (Terre Cuite). These are sold at Leroy Merlin and the hypermarket at vastly cheaper prices than in the UK. For instance a window box of 50x 17cm is around FF24.95 (£3.10) in Continent and £12.99 in the UK.

Glassware

Duralex, Luminarc and Cristal D'Arques are names you may already be familiar with. They are available at the hypermarkets at prices that are at least 20% less than in the UK !

You can also visit the Cristal d'Arques factory in Arques, at avenue du Général de Gaulle, Arques 62510, (Tel: 00 33 3 21 93 00 00) where there is a small museum and a visitor centre where you can make your purchases. The prices here are generally about 10% less than the French retail outlets, but you do have to call in advance.

Lace (Dentelles)

One of the local industries of Calais is Lace making. If you have read the 'Calais Sights' section, you will see that the French take their lace so seriously that there is a museum in Calais to display it. Purchasing lace in France is not always cheaper, but you do get a wider choice.

Look out for the specialist lace shops called dentellières.

Other Shopping Ideas

Garden Furniture
(Jardinage)
Garden furniture is often half the UK price of the equivalent and tempting to buy - but you will need a lot of space in your car! At Leroy Merlin (next to Auchan), Auchan, Continent, Carrefour and Auchan, there is a good selection of both plastic and pine table and chair sets.

Plastic chairs start from FF19.95 (£2.50) and plastic tables 85cm in diameter from as little as FF119.00 (£14.90). A pine table and chair set can be found for only FF599.00 (£75.00).

Pushchairs & Prams
We have received a number of letters about pushchairs and prams. Apparently these are cheaper in the hypermarkets. We have not yet substantiated these claims. If you do let us know.

Light Bulbs
Not a huge saving to be made, but 15% is enough to bring a little light.

Nintendo 64
A visit to Toys R Us in Cité Europe may pay dividends.

When this guide was written a Nintendo 64 cost FF999 which at FF9 to £1 equates to £111.00. Toys R Us in the UK have the same game station for sale at £149.00, that is a difference of £38.00!

Mario Kart game costs FF399, £44.33 in France, in the UK it costs £59.99.

Eating Out

Everything stops for lunch in France. Take time out to enjoy a pastime the French take very seriously - eating!

You know lunchtime has arrived in France when you see the sign **'fermé'** (closed) on shop doors. As the shops and factories close, the restaurants open for business, offering a wide variety of cuisine and ambience.

Choosing a restaurant is easy as they generally display their menus outside. Steer clear though, of empty restaurants - in our experience, they generally deserve to be so!

If you have booked a table at a restaurant, be sure to be on time, as your table is unlikely to be saved for you for more than ten minutes, especially on Sundays, when everyone likes to eat out **en famille.**

Most restaurants cater for the tourists by offering a **menu touristique** usually written in English or with an English translation, alongside the more regional dishes. This usually proves to be good value for money and comprises such dishes as steak and French fries.

One item that will be missing from any French menu is the traditional two-slices-of-bread British sandwich. You may find it referred to on the menu at cafés or brasseries, but it will never be served in sliced bread. The most popular 'sandwich' is the **croque monsieur** which is basically ham and cheese in a **ficelle** (a slimmer version of a **baguette**). There is also a feminine version of this known as **croque-madame** which comes with a fried egg as well.

Alternatively, you could choose the **Prix Fixé** menu, a set price menu which may include the plat du jour (dish of the day) or **spécialité de la maison** (house special). These are a better choice for those wishing to try a more local dish, usually seafood or frogs legs, **cuisses de**

grenouilles. For extra choice you could experiment with the **à la carte** menu or indulge yourself in the **menu gastronomique** for finer quality food.

Not all prices will be highlighted on the menu. The letters **SG** may sit alongside some dishes and stand for **selon grosseur** (according to weight). This applies to dishes that, for practical purposes, are sold by weight, such as lobster or fish. In this instance it is advisable to find out the price before you order.

If the words **service compris** (service included) or service et **taxes compris** (service and taxes included) are on the menu, that means the prices include a service charge. However, odd coins are usually left for the waiter. Otherwise, it is customary to leave a tip of around 10 per cent.

Meals are never rushed in restaurants. This is true even if you only want a snack and a drink at one of the many cafés. You can while away the time at your leisure and this is totally acceptable. However if your are eating to a deadline, pay for your meal when it arrives, as catching the waiter's eye later may prove a challenge.

Tip:
Go for French food while in France. This not only adds to the French experience, but also makes good economic sense; traditional British food and drink such as tea, Scotch whisky and gin or a plate of bacon and eggs are expensive. So check out the menu or 'tarif des consommations' (if in a café or bar) for something that tickles your palate and accompany it with wine (vin ordinaire) or draught beer (pression).

Alternatively French spirits and soft drinks are generally inexpensive relative to their British counterparts on the menu.

Eating Out

Tip:
When ordering coffee, be specific and say exactly what you would like. Unlike British restaurants, just ordering a coffee will not do. The exception to this is during the breakfast meal when coffee is served in large wide-mouthed coffee cups - specially designed for dunking - and milk is a standard accompaniment.

Coffee Styles.

Un café, s'il vous plaît
You will receive an espresso coffee, strong and black in a small espresso cup

Un café au lait s'il vous plaît
You will receive an espresso coffee with milk on the side.

Une crème s'il vous plaît
You will receive a small white coffee

Une crème grande s'il vous plaît
You will receive a white coffee served in normal size cup.

Terms on a French Menu

Les Viandes	Meat
L'agneau	Lamb
Assiette Anglaise	Plate of cold meat
Bifteck haché	Hamburger
Contrefilet	Sirloin
Entrecôte	Steak
Foie	Liver
Foie gras	Goose liver
Faux filet	Sirloin Steak
Jambon	Ham
Langue	Tongue
Rognons	Kidneys

Les Poissons	Fish
Anchois	Anchovy
Anguille	Eel
L'Assiette de fruits de mer	Sea food platter
L'Assiette Nordique	Smoked fish platter
Crevette grise	ShrimpCrevette
Crevette rose	Prawn
Fruit de mer	Shellfish
Gamba	Large prawn
Homard	Lobster
Huître	Oyster
Limand	Lemon sole
Saumon	Salmon
Thon	Tuna
Truite	Trout
Truite arc en ciel	Rainbow trout

Volaille	**Poultry**
Canard	Duck
Dindon	Turkey
Oie	Goose
Faisan	Pheasant
Perdreau	Partridge
Pigeon	Pigeon
Poulet	Chicken (roast)
Poularde	Chicken (boiled)
Poussin	Spring chicken

Sauce	**Sauce**
Béarnaise	Sauce from egg yolks, shallots, wine & tarragon
Béchamel	White sauce with herbs
Beurre blanc	Loire sauce with butter, wine and shallots
Beurre noir	Blackened butter
Meunière	Butter & lemon sauce

Miscellaneous	
Braisé	Braised
Brochette	Skewer
Brouillade	Stew with oil
Brouillé	Scrambled
Fumé	Smoked
Gratinée	Grill browned
Grillé	Grilled
Suprème	Chicken breast or game bird
Terrine	Coarse paté

RESTAURANTS

The following are some suggested places to eat. Remember that lunch time meals are generally served between 12 noon-3.00 pm.

CALAIS

Aquar' aile
Plage de Calais
Fine seafood restaurant
Per head: FF90-FF230
Special offer: On presentation of your guide, a brandy or a tipple to round off the meal.

La Braserade
8 Rue Jean de Vienne
Calais
Carvery style & menu
Per head: FF98-170

Cafe de Champagne
46 rue de la Mer
Calais
Pizza, steak, eggs, loud music
Per head: FF25-60

Château Tilques
Off N42, 10kms before St Omer Calais
Stylish restaurant and hotel
Special offer: On presentation of your guide you will receive a glass of Kir.

Le Détroit
7 Boulevard Ld Résistance
Calais
Fish, seafood
Per head: From FF100

Les Dunes
48 Route National
Bleriot Plage
Calais
Seafood
Per head: From FF100
Special offer: On presentation of your
guide, a bottle of
wine to take home

La Goulu
26 rue de la Mer
Calais
Grill - steaks
Per head: From FF80

Le Grand Bleu
8 rue Jean-Pierre Avron
Bassin de la Colonne (opp. Calais
port)
Calais
Fish, seafood
Per Head: From FF100
Special offer: On presentation of your
guide, choose between cheese or a
glass of wine as an aperitif.

Le Milano
14 Place d'Armes
Calais
The only Pizzeria in the area
Per head: From FF75
Special offer: On presentation of your
guide, a free glass of white wine

Three excellent restaurants
off the D940

Le Thomé de Gamond
Mont Hubert
Escalles
Seafood
Per head: From FF100

Epicure
1 rue de la Gare
Wimereux
Seafood
Per head: From FF125

Restaurant du Cap
Place de la Mairie
Escalles, Cap Blanc-Nez
Seafood
Per head: FF89

BOULOGNE

Chez Fidéline
24 rue du Pot d'Etain
Boulogne
French cuisine
Per head: From FF51

Chez Jules
8 place Dalton
Boulogne
Seafood
Per head: From FF100

Christophe et Laurence
10 rue Coquelin
Boulogne
Deli, steak, brasserie
Per head: FF75

Le Doyen
1 Rue do Doyen
Boulogne
French, candle-lit
Per head: From FF90

La Houblonnière
8 rue Monsigny
Boulogne
Brasseroe style French cuisine
Per head: From FF65

L'Union de la Marine
18 Bd Gambetta
Boulogne
Seafood
Per head: From FF65

135

Le Détroit
7 Bld la Résistance
Calais
Tel: 03 21 34 43 10

Restaurant

" *Le Détroit* "

Per Head: From £11.00
Cuisine: Fish, seafood
Open 12pm-3pm and 6pm-11pm
Special offer for Channel Hopper's. One glass of house white wine on presentation of this guide

La Goulu
26 rue de la Mer
62100 Calais
Tel: 03 21 96 16 52

Per Head: From £8.00
Cuisine: Grill - steaks
Open: 12pm-3pm and 7.30pm-11pm. Closed on Wednesdays.

LA BRASERADE GRILL

La Braserade Grill
8 rue Jean de Vienne
Calais
Tel: 03 21 97 02 59

Cuisine: French
Open daily except Saturday 12pm-4pm and 7pm-midnight

Buffet available at 98FF including as much red wine as you want.

Le Grand Bleu
8 rue Jean-Pierre Avron
Bassin de La Colonne (opposite the port)
Calais
Tel: 03 21 97 97 98

Per Head: From £13.00
English spoken
Cuisine: Fish, seafood
Special offer for Channel Hoppers. Choose between complimentary cheese or a glass of wine.

Restaurant Les Dunes
48 Route National
Bleriot Plage
Tel: 03 21 34 54 30

Cuisine: Seafood
Special offer for Channel Hoppers.
A bottle of wine to take home on presentation of the guide.
From the port take the A16 autoroute and exit at junction (sortie) 14.

Le Milano
14 Place d'Armes
Calais
Tel: 03 21 34 41 20
Open daily 12-2.30 and 7pm-11pm

The only Pizzeria in Calais. Pizzas made the old fashioned way.
Special offer for Channel Hoppers. A free glass of white wine on presentation of the guide.

Hotels

If you are looking to stay overnight or longer, look no further than one of France's best kept secrets. In recent years several chains of budget hotels have been set up on an unmanned auto-check-in basis. Entrance is by credit card through a 'hole in the wall' using the language of your choice, and you can gain access all day and night. The rooms are clean and modern and usually comprise one double and one single bed (bunk style) plus a colour TV with UK channels. A Continental style self-service breakfast is available and usually costs around £2.50 extra per person.

The Formule 1 hotel is exceptionally good value at around £18 per night for up to 3 people. Incredibly, the tariffs in France are based on the room per night and not - as in the UK - per person. Unfortunately there is no en-suite bathroom and the only shower and toilet is a communal one located along the hallway.

Mister Bed, is a slightly more expensive hotel in a similar style but it does include an en-suite shower room. These type of hotels are very popular so book in advance.

CALAIS
Formula 1 Hotel
Ave Charles de Gaulle
Chemin de Bernieulles
62231 Coquelles
Tel: (00 33) (0) 3 21 96 89 89
Near to Auchan Hypermarket. Situated 2km from Eurotunnel. From the ferry port take A26, Autoroute A16, direction Boulogne, exit Junction 12 (sortie 12) Coquelles. Approx. 10 minutes drive.

BOULOGNE
Formula 1 Hotel
Z.I. de l'Inquétrie
Rue Pierre Martin
St Martin Les Boulogne
Tel: (00 33) (0) 3 21 31 26 28
Opposite Auchan Hypermarket. From Calais and Boulogne take N1 to St. Omer A26, exit (sortie) ZI Inquétrie. From St Omer, A26 to Boulogne, exit (sortie) ZI Inquétrie.

ST OMER
Mister Bed Hotel
ZAC du Lobel - N43, 62510 Arques
Tel: (00 33) (0) 3 21 93 81 20
Near the Crystal D'Arques factory. From Calais take A26, exit 3 to St Omer onto N42 then follow signs to Arques- Lille via the Rocade. At the roundabout with N43 (Arques-Béthune), follow sign to Arques.

Hotels

Of course there are a multitude of hotels all over Calais and Boulogne with varying degrees of luxury and facilities.

One hotel that stands out is **Le Copthorn Hotel** in the village of Coquelles in Calais. A three star hotel of modern design with all the trimmings of a four star hotel - short of a porter. Madame Ganier explained her resistence to upgrading 'we are happy with our tariffs, if we upgrade we will be obliged to increase them'.

Sound reasoning, and why this hotel represents such good value at around £58.00 per room per night for two people.

Copthorne have an in-house health club called 'Cap Forme' which the locals use for a membership fee. However, all guests are welcome to use the swimming pool, gym, solarium, sauna and use the ricochet court (this two player game is similar to squash) at no extra cost. You can also eat at Le Copthorne's Le Vieux Moulin. The cuisine is a mix of local French and international dishes, and the Bar Coquelles offer a relaxing atmosphere to enjoy a drink.

Another highly recommended hotel is the **Hôtel Cléry**, a delightful country-house hotel located around 9km - 10 minute drive - south of Calais. Owned by Didier and Catherine Legros, two people passionate about their hotel who have created hotel within a most beautiful environment inside and out and at very reasonable rates - from approximately £37 per room for two people per night.

Other hotels of beauty are **Château Cocove**, and **Château Tilques**. Both hotels are in beautifull grounds and make a perfect weekend retreat.

Le Copthorne Hotel

Le Copthorne Hotel Coquelles-Calais
Avenue Charles de Gaulle
62231 Coquelles
Tel: (00 33) (0)3 21 46 60 60 Fax: (00 33) (0)3 21 85 7676

Dine at Le Vieux Moulin and enjoy both local French dishes and international cuisine

All guests can enjoy the health club at no extra cost

The spacious en-suite rooms are complete with a TV coffee/tea facilities and a trouser press.

SPECIAL OFFER
10% discount on the room on presentation of The Channel Hopper's Guide upon arrival

Set in peaceful woodland near Coquelles, this elegant hotel is only 3 minutes from the Channel Tunnel, 10 minutes from the ferry terminal and 5 minutes from the A26 and A16 motorways.

Hotel Cléry

Hotel Cléry***
Château d'Hesdin l'Abbé,
rue du Château 62360 Hesdin l'Abbé
Tel: (00 33) 21 83 19 83 Fax: (00 33) 21 87 52 59

*We would like to offer you more than just a bed to sleep in.
And during your stay with us, if you feel a spirit of serenity, the
sense of well being and contentment, then we have certainly
earned the title of a "Hotel de Charme".*

22 rooms fully renovated in 1997, from 330FF/room.
A restaurant for guests Monday through Friday night.

*It is our work, our passion, and above all, our pleasure.
Catherine and Didier Legros*

20 minutes from Le Shuttle

10 minutes from Boulogne & Hardelot

20 minutes from Le Touquet

1Km from motorway A16 and RN1

direction of Montreuil.

SPECIAL OFFER
A bottle of wine to
take home, on
presentation of
The Channel
Hopper's Guide
offer ends 1st March 1998

Hôtel Château Tilques
Rue du Château
62500 Tilques
Situated on N42, 10kms before
St Omer
Tel: 00 33 (0) 3 21 88 99 99

Le Château de Cocove
62890 Recques-sur-Hem
On D217, 20kms from Calais
Tel: 00 33 (0) 3 21 82 68 29

Holiday Inn Garden Court
Boulevard des Alliés
62100 Calais
See their advertisement
Tel: 00 33 (0) 3 21 34 69 69

Hôtel Cléry
Rue deu Château
62360 Hesdin l'Abbé
RN1 motorway Boulogne-
Montreuil
Tel: 00 33 (0) 3 21 83 19 93

Les Dunes Hotel
48 Route Nationale
62231 Blériot Plage, Calais
Tel: 00 33 (0) 3 21 34 54 30

Hôtel Faidherbe
12 rue du Château
Boulogne
Tel: 00 33 (0) 3 21 31 60 93

Ibis Plage
170 Bd Ste-Beuve
Boulogne
Tel: 00 33 (0) 3 21 30 12 40

Metropole
51 rue Thiers
Boulogne
Tel: 00 33 (0) 3 21 54 30

Sportifs
rue Faidherbe
Boulogne
Tel: 00 33 (0) 3 21 84 07

How Do You Say?

Pleasantries

Nice to meet you	Enchanté
Yes/No	Oui/non
Good Morning/Good Day	Bonjour
How are you?	Ça va
Good Evening/Good Night	Bonsoir/bonne nuit
Good Bye	Au revoir
See you tommorrow/soon	À demain/bientôt
I've go to go now	Il faut que je me sauve
Excuse me	Excusez-moi
Thank you	Merci
You're welcome	Je vous en prie

Being Understood

I don't speak French	Je ne parle pas français
I don't understand	Je ne comprends pas
Do you speak English?	Parlez-vous anglais?
I don't know how to say it in French	Je ne sais pas le dire en français

Eating Out

A table for two please	Une table pour deux, s'il vous plaît
The menu please	Le menu, s'il vous plaît
Do you have a children's menu?	Avez-vous un menu pour les enfants?
We'll take the set menu, please	Nous prendrons le menu, s'il vous plaît
We would like a dessert	Nous aimerions du dessert
The bill please	L'addition, s'il vous plaît
Is service included?	Le service est compris?
Do you accept credit cards?	Acceptez-vous les cartes de crédit?

Hotels

I'd like a single/double room	Je voudrais une chambre pour une personne/deux personnes
I reserved a room in the name of..	J'ai réservé un chambre au nom de..
I confirmed my booking by phone/letter	J'ai confirmé ma réservation par letter téléphone/lettre
My key, please	Ma clé, s'il vous plaît
I shall be leaving tomorrow	Je partirai demain
What time is breakfast/dinner	Le petit déjeuner/Le dîner est à quelle heure?

How Do You Say?

Directions

How do you get to ......?

Comment fait on pour aller à ...?

How long will it take to get there?

Ça prend combien de temps pour y aller

Where is the nearest supermarket/newsagent/deli?

Où est le supermarché/le tabac/la boulangerie le/la plus près?

Can you tell me how to get to the comment on hotel?

Pouvez-vous me dire fait pour aller à l'hôtel

Where are the toilets?

Où sont les toilettes?

Where's the nearest post box?

Où est la plus proche boîte à lettres?

Where's the nearest phone box?

Où se trouve la cabine téléphonique la plus proche?

Is this the right bus for ...?

C'est bien l'autobus pour... ?

Paying

How much is it?

Ça coûte Combien?

I can't afford to buy it

Je n'ai pas les moyens de l'acheter

I'd like to pay please

On veut payer, s'il vous plaît

Can I have the bill please?

L'addition, s'il vous plaît

Can I pay by credit card? carte de credit?

Puis-je payer avec une

Do you accept traveller's cheques/Eurocheques/Sterling?

Acceptez-vous les cheques de voyages/Eurocheques/Sterling?

Telephoning

I would like to make a phone call

Je voudrais appeler

I would like Directory Enquiries

Je voudrais les renseignements

I would like to reverse the charges (PCV is pronounced pay say vay)

Je voudrais téléphoner en PCV

Can I speak to...?

Est-ce que je peux parler à ...

I've been cut off

Nous avons été coupés

I can't get through

Je n'arrive pas àobtenir a communication

You may hear:

Ne quittez pas!

I'm trying to connect you, hold the line

Je vous le passe

I'm putting you through

Je suis désolée, mais la ligne est occupée

I'm sorry it's engaged

C'est de la part de qui?

Who's calling

Ce n'est pas le bon numéro

Sorry, wrong number